THE BINDING OF ISAAC

THE BINDING OF ISAAC

Reading Behind the Lines

ANTHONY RUDOLF

Printed by imprintdigital
Upton Pyne, Exeter
www.digital.imprint.co.uk

Typesetting and cover design by The Book Typesetters
us@thebooktypesetters.com
07422 598 168
www.thebooktypesetters.com

Published by Shoestring Press
19 Devonshire Avenue, Beeston, Nottingham, NG9 1BS
(0115) 925 1827
www.shoestringpress.co.uk

First published 2021

ISBN 978-1-912524-85-3

THE BINDING OF ISAAC

followed by

ISAAC ROSENBERG IN HEAVEN

(with Scene One from

NOBODY'S ROMEO)

For John Lucas

To the memory of Jon Silkin and Owen Lowery

What is happening to me now is more tragic than the 'passion play'. Christ never endured what I endure. It is breaking me completely.

– *Isaac Rosenberg*

Poetry's task is not only to express the matter in hand but also to add to the stock of available reality.

– *R. D. Blackmur*

Life contracts, and death is expected.

– *Wallace Stevens* ('The Death of a Soldier')

PREFATORY NOTE

Some of the sections have been worked up from notes I prepared for a University of Leeds Poetry Centre round table, which was part of the Isaac Rosenberg centenary celebration held on November 29 2018. Some are new and reflect more recent reading and thought. Some have been revised or amplified from previous writings.

I begin with a group of scene-setting epigraphs from Rosenberg and end with the first scene of my "play", which is inspired by my perhaps faulty memory of *Rameau's Nephew* and other philosophical dialogues by Diderot.

All or almost all books referred or quoted from are listed in the bibliography, although mainly not indicated in the main text.

a) And when he calls unto the stars of paradise with heaven-sweet songs
To his divided self he calls and sings the story of earth's wrongs. (? Autumn, 1912)

If poetry at this time is no use, it certainly won't be at any other (letter to Edward Marsh, July 30 2016)

b) *Lilith*
I think there is more sorrow in the world
Than man can bear

Nubian
None can exceed their limit, lady.
You either bear or break.
(from *The Amulet*,1917)

c) …Never have I reached
The halfway of the purpose I have planned
(from 'Raphael', 1912)

None saw their spirits' shadow shake the grass
Or stood aside for the half-used life to pass
(from 'Dead Man's Dump', 1917)

d) The roots' hid secrecy, old source of race,
Unreasoned reason of the savage instinct.
(from *Moses*, 1916)

Caught still as Absolom
……………………………..
We are lifted of all we know
And hang from implacable boughs
(first and last two lines of 'Chagrin')

e) Music was articulate feeling. The inexpressible in poetry, in painting, was there expressed.
(undated letter to Winifreda Seaton)

……. Strange wine
of some large knowledge
(from 'Day')

CONTENTS

LIST OF ILLUSTRATIONS

Part One: The Binding of Isaac

1) ISAAC ROSENBERG'S *SELF-PORTRAIT WITH A STEEL HELMET*

> They see with living eyes
> How long they have been dead

Self-Portrait with a Steel Helmet, made in gouache and chalk "on brown wrapping paper" (from a package to him?), is a finished work, perhaps Isaac Rosenberg's final visual work. The key word is "finished". It has the classic Rosenberg look, steely, yet ironic and quizzical. Rosenberg's sister Annie Wynick, in her brief memoir written soon after the war, claimed that the picture was done "in the Trenches". This was a widespread and sometimes misleading way of saying "at the front". The self-portrait was made in July 1916, perhaps as early as June – after the issue of steel helmets at the front – given that it is "finished" and would have needed time and space to be executed. In a letter to Sir Edward Marsh dated August 4, 1916, the poet encloses a draft of 'Break of Day in the Trenches' and states that he has "been given a job behind the lines and very rarely go into the trenches". He would have worked on the self-portrait in a billet where clerical work was done, rather than in the cramped dug-out shown in other pencil sketches. In a letter to Robert Trevelyan written some time between June and August 1916, Rosenberg states that on "the other side of this sheet is a very crude sketch of how I look here in this dugout".

Given Rosenberg's circumstances, that he wrote poems at all – as well as making sketches and self-portraits – is a tribute to his fortitude, self-discipline and tough-mindedness.

The self-portrait represents a moment of truth, a sense of a beginning, a more objective approach. We know with hindsight that death will never be the same again after World War One. One of the reasons we know this is that the poets of war, Isaac Rosenberg at the very pinnacle, bore witness in extreme circumstances and bequeathed us the legacy of their work.

According to Robert Manne, recent scholarship shows that at

least 150,000 Jews were murdered in pogroms in the bloodlands of Eastern Europe between 1919 and 1921, a prefiguration of the Holocaust and a direct outcome of World War One. I would argue that the use of poison gas by both sides in World War One and other modalities of industrialised mass death, created one of the pathways, perhaps the central pathway, which led eventually to Auschwitz and Hiroshima, a subject I have touched on elsewhere[1]. André Malraux's account of the use of poison gas on the Eastern Front in 1915 can be found in *The Walnut Trees of Altenburg*, written during World War Two at the very moment the Final Solution was being planned and before Malraux joined the Resistance. (It is reprinted in his *Lazarus* in a more personal context). This work has unexpected affinities with David Jones's *In Parenthesis*, as John Matthias points out in his fascinating new book, *Some Words on Those Wars*, where memoir and literary criticism/history overlap. Writing about World War One after World War Two, one cannot fail to be influenced by the history and representations of the latter.

1. For this paragraph, see additionally notes included in the Bibliography at the end of the book, under 'Rudolf 1990' and 'HM Government Integrated Review 2021' (the latter in the Online section of the bibliography). See also the listing of the Hungarian-born artist Gyula Zilzer (and the acknowledgment to Peter Redman). As in the rest of the book, the sources of all citations can be found in the bibliography. One of Zilzer's lithographs is reproduced on page 58. Ivor Gurney (more on him in later sections) suffered from the effects of a gas shell.

2) ISAAC ROSENBERG AND KEITH DOUGLAS

Keith Douglas, who died at the age of twenty-four in World War Two, had such a radical access to his vision that he bears comparison with Isaac Rosenberg, whom he alludes to in several places and apostrophises in a key poem written a year before he died, 'Desert Flowers': "Rosenberg I only repeat what you were saying", an eloquently modest understatement of the influence, indeed indebtedness. Had Rosenberg survived, he would have already written his great poems of the war. The Anglo-Welsh poet, David Jones, wrote his magnum opus – *In Parenthesis* – long after the war, and one may suppose that he and Isaac Rosenberg would have entered into some kind of dialogue of equals, if only on the page. Private Isaac Rosenberg (22311) of the Bantams, 12th Suffolk Battalion, subsequently drafted into the Kings Own Royal Lancaster Regiment – like Jones a poet and painter and non-officer – wrote poetry in the trenches, such as 'Break of Day in the Trenches' itself, and even made some pencil sketches there. Another non-officer poet, the composer Ivor Gurney, also wrote poems in the trenches. Composing music in such circumstances was almost impossible.

Keith Douglas was a precocious, mature and fastidious poet. He describes his own approach as "extrospective", an approach itself explored extrospectively by the late poet Owen Lowery in his fascinating university thesis on Douglas, and in many of his own poems too. Owen, a tetraplegic with his health always on the front line, identified with Keith Douglas. A prime quality, *de rigueur* if you are going to write poems in the trenches that will later be regarded as great is to be.... extrospective – and this quality, virtue indeed, we find in Rosenberg's poems and letters. Thus, in an undated letter of 1916 to Mrs Herbert Cohen (Jennie Salaman Cohen), he writes that the war should be approached "in a colder way, more abstract, with less of the million feelings everybody feels; or all these should be concentrated in one distinguished emotion".

3) ISAAC ROSENBERG AND EZRA POUND AND AN INVENTION

In his *ABC of Reading*, Ezra Pound quotes Basil Bunting as having discovered the equation "dichten = condensare.... while fumbling about with a German-Italian dictionary". However doubtful the etymology, this was, Pound wrote, Bunting's "prime contribution to contemporary criticism". *Dichten* involves one word where in English we need three: "to compose poetry". The poetics underlying the equation has been hugely influential. I have by heart two sentences Isaac Rosenberg wrote to Lawrence Binyon in autumn 1916 (exact date unknown): "I am determined that this war, with all its powers for devastation, shall not master my poeting; that is, if I am lucky enough to come through all right. I will not leave a corner of my consciousness covered up". He uses the verb form "... my poeting...", which clearly derives from a non-existent verb in English: "to poet". Rosenberg's first language, Yiddish, employs the same single word as German, namely *dichten*, and this could be the source of Rosenberg's invention. The poet and novelist Elizabeth Cook, who led the campaign for a plaque to Rosenberg at the Whitechapel Public Library, is reminded of the beginning of Psalm 45: "My heart is inditing a good matter".

Isaac Rosenberg met T. E. Hulme in 1913 and Yeats in late 1914 at the Café Royal. It was Yeats who alerted Pound to Rosenberg's poetry, despite considering much of it "windy and rhetorical". Rosenberg corresponded with Pound, who brokered his publication in *Poetry Chicago*, and met him at least once in Hulme's circle, a circle he had access to thanks to the well-connected and generous Sir Edward Marsh, who was Churchill's private secretary at the Admiralty and an admirer and mentor of Rosenberg, despite their differing poetics.

4) ISAAC ROSENBERG AND JON SILKIN

In the letter to Edward Marsh, dated August 4, 1916, cited earlier, Rosenberg writes: "I have a fine idea for a most gorgeous play, Adam and Lilith". By October he tells Marsh that he has started work on it. But he abandons it for a drama about a non-biblical couple (despite the overtones) named Lilith and Saul, *The Amulet*, which he describes in a letter to Marsh of May 1917, asking him not to read a fragment sent earlier (premature private disclosure to confidants is a *déformation professionelle* common among poets, something made worse in our day by the speed and ease of emailing). *The Amulet* would morph into *The Unicorn.* There is too another drama Rosenberg plans to write, which he mentions twice in letters: first in the 1916 letter to Mrs Cohen already quoted: "I am thinking of a Jewish play, with Judas Macabeas [*sic*]" and in the autumn 1916 letter to Binyon about "poeting": "I have thought of a play around our Jewish hero, Judas Maccabeus". (Despite his support for Rosenberg, Binyon did not include him alongside Owen and Newbolt in his 1924 edition of *Palgrave's Golden Treasury*).

Rosenberg's mythical verse dramas have been under-rated, although not by Robert Graves, as Deborah Maccoby points out in her discussion of one of the poet's great works, *Moses* (symbolising freedom from slavery, as Rosenberg says in a letter to Robert Trevelyan), and also *The Unicorn.* The unicorn, in turn, symbolises, as Rosenberg wrote in a letter to his friend and mentor, Winifreda Seaton, "the war and all the devastating forces let loose by an ambitious and unscrupulous will" (March 8, 1918).

Before finding his mature voice, Rosenberg saturated himself in and mimicked English poetry, from Marvell and Donne to his Georgian contemporaries via a prime source, Keats, whom he read endlessly in the Whitechapel Public Library. This was essential for a serious and ambitious poet, not least if he was going to write in his second language.

As a critic, Jon Silkin wrote with commitment, empathy and high intelligence about the war poets, in particular Isaac

Rosenberg; *Out of Battle* is a major critical study of their work. Rosenberg's syntax and diction, influenced by the Yiddish he heard at home and all round him in Bristol and the East End of London before he headed for the trenches, plainly (i.e. colourfully) influenced Silkin. When Silkin deals with his own Jewishness in verse, he appears, perhaps paradoxically, less tangled up in the very roots of language than in his other poems: his struggle with the 'enabling angel' was gentler, the thought was clearer, the tone less combative.

Silkin wrote some of the strongest Jewish poems (poems, that is, which wrestle with theological and existential dilemmas of Jewishness, not at all poems which merely happen to be written by a Jew) of any Anglo-Jewish poet since the relevant poems of Isaac Rosenberg. Among Silkin's Jewish poems are 'Footsteps on A Downcast Path', a lengthy meditation on Jewish victimhood and martyrdom, 'A Word about Freedom and Identity in Tel-Aviv', 'Resting Place', 'Two Poems Concerning Jews in England' and 'The Life of a Poet'. The last-named poem is dedicated to Rosenberg and, like Keith Douglas's poem, addressed to Rosenberg.

5) ISAAC ROSENBERG, JON SILKIN/JON GLOVER AND URI ZVI GREENBERG

.........................Ah, if only I could bear up
the cup of bitterness,
my eyes turned inward, I would drink to the terror in the eyes
of soldiers, brothers whom I fought with
and reached the Sawa's water.

They fell, tangled on the wire,
their feet raised high,
and that wail, essence of their dying, lasted only
a moment; they died, then,
very dark.
....
....
This fearful glowing on the nails in the boots of the dead
who kick at God.....

– Uri Zvi Greenberg (extract from 'Naming Souls')

The prologue to the essential anthology edited by Jon Silkin and Jon Glover, the *Penguin Book of First World War Prose*, is the only poem in the whole book and as such stands out. 'Naming Souls' by Uri Zvi Greenberg, translated by Silkin and Ezra Spicehandler, was written in Hebrew, which suggests it was written after the war, since Greenberg's early poems were written in Yiddish. And yet the expressionist tone and the powerful immediacy suggest proximity in time and place. It is the only poem in Hebrew or Yiddish by Greenberg which directly refers to World War One. Born in my own grandfather's native East Galicia (now West Ukraine) in 1896 and thus a few years younger than Rosenberg, Greenberg published his first book of Yiddish poems in 1915 when he was drafted into the Austrian army – from which he deserted in 1917. He was in the trenches and briefly saw front-line action on the Serbian front. Later he was a courier on horseback between regiments (My grandfather was a messenger between regiments in an earlier generation). The poet, who grew up in L'wow (now L'viv), close enough to my ancestral town of Stanislawow, left Europe for Mandate Palestine in 1923 (Israel from 1948) and lived there until he died in 1981, apart from a number of years spent in Poland in the 1930s, where he was editing a Zionist magazine.[2]

'Naming Souls', first published in a book in 1928, has distinct affinities with well known war poems written in English. In Jon Silkin's view, this is not surprising, "so consistent and characteristic is the poetry of war". Certainly there is no question of influence in either direction. 'Naming Souls' shares with Rosenberg the traditional Jewish agon toward God that such a war would generate in a common soldier, or in an officer for that matter. In his later years, responding to the two world wars, Greenberg would become a conservative nationalist, indeed a ferocious right-wing Revisionist Zionist, almost unique among the poets and writers. Isaac Rosenberg's poems, translated by Ya'acov Orland, were not published in Hebrew until 1998, according to the Jerusalem poet, Miriam Neiger. Joseph Leftwich translated some of his friend's poems into Yiddish for the benefit of the poet's father but, as this book went to press, even with the help of experts I have not succeeded in establishing the publication of Yiddish translations, whether by Leftwich or anyone else. Thus, six issues of the Yiddish literary magazine *Renesans*, edited by the poet Leo Konig, were published in London in 1920 and in the contents pages which I was able to check, there is, somewhat surprisingly, no listing of Isaac Rosenberg. Rosenberg did make illustrations, now lost, of poems by London Yiddish poets such as Konig.

2. The whole question of Israel/Palestine as a territorial and political conflict is not touched on in *The Binding of Isaac.* (Nor is there any reason to do so, given the time line). This does not affect the arguments in the book. I have written about the conflict in several forums over the years including a chapter in the collection *A Time to Speak Out.*(bibliography, 2007, Rudolf).

6) ISAAC ROSENBERG AND JOSEPH LEFTWICH

Joseph Leftwich and Isaac Rosenberg were close friends and contemporaries, members of the group of poets and painters known as the Whitechapel Boys. Leftwich (1892–1984), whose posthumously published poems I reviewed long ago, left a diary for 1911/1912, an important document which ought to be edited and published. On the first day of the Jewish New Year in 2021, I read both a published lecture Leftwich gave on Zangwill and Rosenberg and parts of the unpublished diary, a photocopy of which is kept in a place I always enjoy going to, the Tower Hamlets Local History Library and Archives in Bancroft Road, next door to Queen Mary College. I mention this detail because on the same festival in 1911, Leftwich told his father he was going to attend a different synagogue that morning, but instead bunked off to the National Gallery, a typical destination for someone in his high-minded circle of autodidacts. This was an invisible rebellion, which I understand very well. Leftwich went on to become a man of letters, a critic and translator, and an anthologist of Jewish and Yiddish poets. He was a modest and decent man, with no illusions about his standing as poet, especially when compared with the one to whose genius he deferred all his life. He was proud when someone mistook his memorial poem to Rosenberg as a poem by Rosenberg himself, a poem which ended up in an anthology edited by Edmund Blunden. In the diary Leftwich describes how Rosenberg was interviewed informally and accepted as a member of the group which also included John Rodker, later to become a significant modernist poet himself, and publisher of a complete edition of Freud in German as well as an important poetry list.

"Poetry is his passion" writes Leftwich of Rosenberg. "When we get to the corner of Jamaica Street and Oxford Street. Rosenberg pulls a bundle of odd scraps of paper out of his pocket, and reads us his poems under a lamp-post. The fellow writes really good poetry". The group had issues with his awkward and unsociable personality but, to their credit, they welcomed him and shared Leftwich's view of his significance as a poet, although Leftwich was not impressed by the drawings and paintings Rosenberg showed him – and another member, Simon Winsten – in the kitchen of the flat where the poet lived with his parents and siblings in dire poverty. However, all the boys including Leftwich later admired a large self-portrait. One cannot overestimate the importance of the group for Rosenberg, who matured in their company over the years.

We learn that the painter Solomon J. Solomon (of whom more later) urged Rosenberg to take up painting for a career but Rosenberg was dubious, needing regular income to supplement his father's low earnings as a poetry-loving pedlar and the small income from fine needlework which his mother Hacha, as Jean Moorcroft Wilson explains, would peddle to smart Jewish ladies uptown after the failure of her sweetshop stocked with home-made confectionary and ice-cream from recipes given by neighbours. See the letter to Lawrence Binyon from the artist Frank Emanuel (in 2007 Jean Liddiard), urging Rosenberg to "learn an art trade". Israel Zangwill too had tried to encourage Rosenberg during the seven years Isaac was working at the Fleet Street studios of the fine-art engraver Carl Hentschel, whom Zangwill – once so famous himself – knew through Jerome K. Jerome. Zangwill told Isaac's sister Annie: "you can tell your brother from me that there are a good many beautiful and powerful lines". After the war, when Annie, a key figure in the posthumous life-support of Rosenberg's work, asked Leftwich to become Isaac's literary executor, he rightly said no on grounds of age and recommended Ian Parsons and Patric Dickinson.

F.R. Leavis is quoted by Leftwich as saying that "there are a dozen pages of great poetry. Genius is the word for Rosenberg". Leftwich also quotes Edith Sitwell as saying: "He was one of the greatest poets we have had in this or the last generation. I do not care to think what such a poet might have become and what we have lost". Jean Liddiard tells me that Leavis used to say (this was when she was a student at Cambridge in the early sixties, my exact contemporary although we never met) that the only war poet he still read was Rosenberg.

7) ISAAC ROSENBERG AND AVROM NOKHEM STENCL AND MY FAMILY

The best known Londoner to write poetry in Yiddish was Avrom Nokhem Stencl. He lived and wrote in his adopted shtetl Whitechapel after leaving his native Poland and Weimar Germany. Here he edited his magazine *Loshn un Lebn* (Language and Life) and, indeed, sold me a copy outside the public library (now part of the Whitechapel Gallery), where Rosenberg had studied. This was where my uncle Jack met my aunt Fan, my mother's older sister (who was born in Rodinsky's not-yet-famous room above the synagogue in Princelet Street), at the beginning of their eighty-four-year relationship. Both Rosenberg and Stencl were published and printed by Narod Press at 48 Mile End Road. My paternal grandfather Joseph Rudolf, then a trouser maker and later a dealer in second-hand clothes and army surplus, lived and worked close to the various Isaac Rosenberg addresses. Could Isaac or his parents have met Joseph? Might our family name have given Rosenberg the name of the character Rudolph (nobody ever spells the name right) in the eponymous partly autobiographical story fragment by Rosenberg? Other coincidences: my mother was born Esther Rosenberg (a common enough Jewish surname in Poland) and Isaac's sister Annie's married name was Wynick, my grandmother Rebecca Rosenberg's maiden name: this is a less common name. If our Wynick families had been from the same town, I would doubtless be related by marriage to Isaac, but my grandmother was from Vashlikova, a shtetl near Bialystock (Belarus and now Poland) and I learn in an email from Rosenberg's surviving nephew Bernard Wynick that the name had been changed from Wainik, and that they were from Lithuania, not Poland. But I am overdoing the "iffing". If my grandmother had had wheels she would have been a trolley-bus, as my father used to say – probably updating a Yiddish phrase – when I was engaging in the habit.

8) ISAAC ROSENBERG AND THE NATIONAL GALLERY

In Rosenberg's cosmopolitan often droll story *Rudolph*, the main character meets a woman in the National Gallery who is "painting the interior and you just happen to fit in well". He looks at the picture and comments that it is "Dutch in idea and influence and yet exceedingly modern". I wonder if one of the National Gallery Van Eycks, perhaps *The Arnolfini Portrait*, is implied as being included along with Rudolph in this fictional interior, since the woman or rather lady tells him that Van Eyck is the greatest painter who ever lived. Rudolph concedes that Van Eyck is interesting but tells her he prefers Dante Gabriel Rossetti – hardly in Van Eyck's league. Was Rosenberg aware of the now famous association between *The Arnolfini Portrait* and the Pre-Raphaelites? In real life, it was Rosenberg who, on 11 March 1911, was copying *Philip IV* of Velasquez, and discussed painting techniques with the lady who observed him, Mrs Lily Delissa Joseph, although, again, in real life, she herself used to paint regularly in the National Gallery. (A few days after the meeting, he painted a picture for her in the rain on Hampstead Heath). Impressed by his work, the future suffragette, pilot and painter became one of his three sponsors at the Slade School, along with her sister Mrs Henrietta Löwy and Mrs Jennie Salaman Cohen. He wrote the story the following month. While at the Slade, the painter Jacob Kramer, to whom Isaac dedicated a minor poem, a fragment, rescued him when he was being bullied by the Chilean-born student Alvaro Guevara: Kramer later painted the magnificent *Yom Kippur*, now in Leeds City Art Gallery; Guevera made a portrait of Edith Sitwell. When I showed Paula Rego, who studied at the Slade forty years after Rosenberg, reproductions of the poet's paintings, she said: "Very Slade!"

On December 20, 2018, I went with one of Rosenberg's three biographers Jean Liddiard (also editor of two selections of Rosenberg's poems and letters) to the National Gallery. We had made an appointment with the research centre in the gallery library to look at the Copy Registers from around 1911, acting upon information from Colin Wiggins concerning the permissions system – which even in the digital age remains unchanged – for using an easel one day a week, and for which a pass is required. To copy on a drawing pad does not require a pass. We discovered that on March 12 1910 a Mrs Joseph (no initial) had obtained a pass. Her address is given as the Royal Palace Hotel in Kensington, and her referee is Mrs A. Solomon of 46 Finchley Road, perhaps a relative or in-law of the portrait painter Solomon J. Solomon RA, who was Lily Delissa Joseph's brother, and not to be confused with the tragic figure of Simeon Solomon, the Jewish and homosexual pre-Raphaelite. Solomon Solomon always added his initial J, for that reason.

"Mrs Joseph" can only be Lily Delissa Joseph, although why she gave a hotel address is unknown, unless she and her family were moving house or she had a reason for maintaining privacy. The entry number is 18776. Almost a year later to the day, she would meet Rosenberg by chance for their critically important first encounter. Isaac Rosenberg's copy register entry number is 18950 and he obtained his pass on January 27 1911. His address, as we know, was 159 Oxford Street (now Stepney Way, or what remains of it), Mile End. During this time the poet was sitting for a portrait by John Amschewitz and also wrote a Keatsian-inspired sonnet to him, so it is no surprise that Amschewitz is named as his referee, his address being 2 Parkhill Studios, Parkhill Road, Hampstead. The National Gallery evidence for Rosenberg's appropriateness as an artist is given as "specimen" in the "How Admitted" column. Other artists in the register whose names caught our eye were Morris Goldstein, Bernard Meninsky and, on September 6 1913, Mark Gertler, 32 Elder Street.

9) ISAAC ROSENBERG AND JOSEPH POLACK AND A LETTER

Lily Delissa Joseph's niece was Ruth Löwy, daughter of Lily's sister Henrietta Löwy, one of Rosenberg's other two sponsors. Mrs Joseph found work for Rosenberg as art tutor to her sons and their cousins, including Ruth, who was Rosenberg's contemporary at the Slade, and whose portrait he drew in 1912. He also depicted her, pre-Raphaelite style, in *Sleeping Beauty*. Undoubtedly he was attracted to her, but there is no evidence of any romantic connection between the two. She married the future publisher Victor Gollancz in 1919. In the last of Rosenberg's letters (February or March 1917) to Miss Löwy (Rosenberg always employed the formal address, perhaps deferring to her higher status in class terms), he gives us a rare glimpse of his childhood: "I spent my wild little pick a back days in Bristol; was born there, too. I have some vague faraway memories of the name of Polack in connection I fancy with Hebrew classes and prize giving".

This Polack can only have been the Reverend Joseph Polack, born in 1857. Why such a title for a Jewish minister? Because, aping the Church of England, Chief Rabbi Nathan Adler, when he set up Jews College in 1855 – the orthodox seminary in London which Polack attended – ordained (as it were) that graduates of the College could not use the title rabbi and must wear dog collars and canonicals. He was the sole authority on matters of Jewish law. Even as late as the 1960s/1970s I recall that some orthodox Jewish ministers wore dog collars, the last being the Reverend Isaac Livingston in Golders Green. Joseph Polack, who also had a degree in German from London University, was junior minister at the Prince's Road synagogue in Liverpool for two years and chief minister from 1882 till 1890. In that year, he became housemaster of the Jewish house at Clifton College, Bristol, the city where, in 1890, Rosenberg was born into a Yiddish speaking family.

Founded in 1878, the Jewish house became known as Polack's,

the first, last and perhaps unique Jewish house in an English public school. Clifton College was not a place of education the impoverished working class Rosenbergs could aspire to for their sons. Polack was at the centre of Anglophone Jewish life in Bristol for decades and by inference represented a classic example of the Anglo-Jewish symbiosis in cultural and educational terms. He was chairman or president of various communal organisations. By inference, too, he oversaw, and taught at, the Hebrew classes Isaac remembered attending, doubtless in the Park Row synagogue. The future poet was very young, probably six, when he received a prize, given that the family left Bristol for London when he was seven.

Polack was a busy man. He lectured in Hebrew at the University College of Bristol from 1891 (later the University of Bristol), teaching Hebrew and German and perhaps other subjects at Clifton in his early years there, running its Jewish house until 1923 and also Hebrew classes in the Bristol synagogue. We learn from the internet site, *Epitaphs of the Great War*, that Polack himself lost two sons on the field of battle: Ernest, an officer in the Gloucesters, on 17 July 1916 in France, and Benjamin, an officer in the Worcester Regiment, on 9 April 1916 in Basra. Ernest quotes Shakespeare in his surviving letters from the front, and the epigraph chosen by Polack for Ernest quotes Richard III's description of Prince Edward after the latter's death. Polack's wife Sophia died in March 1918, perhaps from illness (Spanish flu?) and certainly a collateral victim of the war. Polack himself lived on till 1932. He must have known about his student's achievements and would have reflected on the tragedy of Isaac's death as well as the deaths of his own two sons two years earlier, within three months of each other.

Benjamin Polack was engaged to be married to "Ruth Löwy". As with Joseph Polack earlier, the inference is inescapable: this is the same Ruth Löwy who was a friend of Rosenberg's and who received the letter quoted above. (And it is on the record that she had a deceased fiancé). The inference confirms that "Polack" is the Reverend Joseph Polack and explains why the words Polack and Bristol come up in a letter apparently out of the blue –

almost a year after the death of her fiancé. There is no hint of condolence, which he would surely have expressed in an earlier letter of his, unmentioned and now sadly lost. Ruth Löwy's uncle, Solomon J. Solomon, painted the portrait of Polack commissioned by the school, which was presented to him on his retirement in 1923. They must have discussed or at least had in mind Polack's sons, as well as Rosenberg and Sir Douglas Haig (see section 13).

According to the *Times* obituary of his grandson Ernest Polack (doubtless named for Ernest's deceased uncle), Joseph Polack was succeeded in turn by his son Albert, nephew of Philip and Ernest. The Jewish house at Clifton survived until 2005, when changing *mores* made its existence superfluous to requirements. (The only Jewish public school Carmel College, in Berkshire then Oxfordshire, closed down in 1997 and many of the students transferred to the Jewish house at Clifton). For years, the poetry of World War One has been an 'A' Level option in English schools.

10) ISAAC ROSENBERG AND EVGENY VINOKUROV

Evgeni Vinokourov's poem 'Eyes' describes a scene that is more reminiscent of the first-hand descriptions of World War One in Rosenberg's 'Dead Man's Dump' than of those by his near-contemporary Keith Douglas, born five years before the Soviet Russian poet.

Rosenberg's own Russian connection: his parents were born in Dvinsk, now in Latvia, then in Lithuania. Lithuania was part of the Russian Empire, from whose army, notoriously cruel to Jews and entirely anti-Semitic, Isaac's father Dovber (Barnett and later Barnard) Rosenberg naturally fled.

At the age of eighteen, in 1943, Zhenya was already a platoon commander on the Ukrainian front. All the men under his command, he told me, were illiterate.

'Eyes'
(translated by Anthony Rudolf)

Exploded. To the ground. On his back. Arms apart. He
Raised himself to his knees, and bit his lips.
Across his face were smeared not tears
But eyes shot out.

Awful awful. Bent double, I heaved
Him to one side. He was all
Covered with clay. I could hardly
Drag him across to the village.

In the field-hospital he cried
To the nurse: 'Oh it hurts! When you change
The bandage it's hell!' And I gave him, as one does,
Something to smoke as he lay dying.

And when (taking him away) the wheels began
To whimper sharply, over all the voices
I suddenly remembered, for the first time:
My friend had pale blue eyes.

11) ISAAC ROSENBERG AND PETER VANSITTART

Peter Vansittart, in his brilliant polyphonic anthology *Voices from the Great War* deploys unexpected and cunning juxtapositions: thus, for example, the Balfour Declaration is surrounded by two passages from Rosenberg. Another Rosenberg extract – "What is happening to me now is more tragic than the 'passion play'. Christ never endured what I endure. It is breaking me completely" (from a letter to Edward Marsh, January 26, 1918) – is immediately followed by Rudyard Kipling's 'Gethsemane', a classically fluent Christian poem, light years from Rosenberg's tone and yet well placed by Vansittart, as always. The Rosenberg sentences were, according to Vivien Noakes's *Isaac Rosenberg*, her scholarly and definitive edition of the poet), excised from the letter by the army censor. Presumably the crossing out faded over the years and the censored words could be read under the erasure. The index reveals that there are more quotes by Vansittart from Rosenberg than any other writer.

12) ISAAC ROSENBERG AND J. L. CARR

A handwritten letter from J.L. Carr, inserted in one of his entertaining mini-dictionaries, states that he is suffering from "cash-flowitis and shall not publish any books for a few months", a benign way of saying no to my suggestion in 1976 that he publish Isaac Rosenberg in his poetry series, in a mini-selection made by me. Coincidentally, he had been reading Rosenberg's biography "only a few months ago". Carr's short novel *A Month in the Country* is a beautiful and moving book about an art restorer damaged by the Great War. I wonder which of the three biographies – by Jean Moorcroft Wilson, Jean Liddiard and Joseph Cohen, all published in 1975 – Carr had been reading.

13) ISAAC ROSENBERG, MARK GERTLER, DAVID BOMBERG AND SOLOMON J. SOLOMON

Mark Gertler was a year younger than David Bomberg and Isaac Rosenberg, who were born ten days apart. The two major painters from Rosenberg's circle came from the same impoverished Polish Jewish background. Gertler grew up in Spitalfields, Bomberg (ex-Birmingham) in Whitechapel, both close to where my maternal grandparents were living at the time. Mark Gertler, John Rodker and Isaac Rosenberg used to meet at Bomberg's studio in Tenter Buildings. In Bomberg's lost pencil drawing of Rosenberg, *Head of a Poet* (reproduced in William Lipke's monograph *David Bomberg*), Isaac appears softer and slightly fleshier than in his self-portraits. By the time of his death, he was already a great poet on the strength of his best verse, but not yet the equal of his two friends as a visual artist. We cannot know whether he would have approached their high achievement. He wrote of himself that he was "more true as a poet than a painter". Frank Auerbach is quoted by Jean Moorcroft Wilson as reporting his teacher Bomberg's judgment that Rosenberg failed to meet the challenge of the new movements in arts[3]. What, in turn, did Isaac think of Bomberg's poems? Had Rosenberg lived, what would he have made of the Vorticist-inflected ultra-stylised expressiveness of Kramer's 'Day of Atonement', painted in 1919? That would have been one of the movements Bomberg was referring to.

Still and all, we can say that we lost a great poet in Rosenberg and may have lost a significant painter. Bomberg went to Palestine to paint from 1923 to 1927. That would have made an

3. I wrote to Frank Auerbach asking him for further thoughts. [See his reply on the next page]. Bomberg's remark about Solomon J.Solomon is incorrect. Rosenberg was not apprenticed to Solomon or indeed to any Royal Academician, only to the engraver Hentschel (see Chapter Six). However, Solomon did recommend that Rosenberg submit a painting to the Academy.

14 September 2021

Dear Tony

Just a small fragment.

I was in David Bomberg's class, aged 16: the class was sparsely attended and there was a certain amount of conversation with Bomberg. He asked me about my life and background, whether I knew any painters, and I mentioned a painter called Archibald Ziegler, whose wife had taught at my boarding school, and who had, among other works, carried out a rather illustrative and circumstantial mural at Toynbee Hall in the early thirties. Apparently he was not wholly approved of, and Bomberg said: "I was at the Slade with a good poet, who was also a good painter – but he became apprenticed to a Royal Academician (I think Solomon J. Solomon) who ruined him as a painter", I (sixteen year old knowall) said: "Do you mean Isaac Rosenberg?" Bomberg, slightly taken aback, said "Yes". The above, full and circumstantial, account is the whole of it.

With good wishes, Frank

PS As to Rosenberg's paintings – possibly a nascent talent for art while the poetry, awkward and ungainly, not at all knowing, seems to me to have elements of grandeur. It certainly sticks in the mind.

impression on Rosenberg, both as a poet and as a painter, and he might have decided to check out Zion, perhaps in the company of his friend. In the Oxford lecture which I draw on for *Nobody's Romeo* later on, Geoffrey Hill makes a comparison between Bomberg's modernist views on grasping mood through mass and structure and Rosenberg's use of language, as opposed to Owen's more conservative approach (cf Sassoon's comment that Rosenberg "modelled" words). Owen, he argues, is inscribed in a long tradition (and not to his advantage), whereas the literary influences on Rosenberg, in Hill's surprising opinion, are not evident. The fact is, Rosenberg transcended his poetical and dramatic influences (Shakespeare, Milton, Donne, Blake, the Romantics especially Keats, the Old Testament) more fully, partly because he himself was a painter, a point Hill could have made.

In a letter to Edward Marsh in August 1916, Rosenberg (better connected in the literary and art worlds than might be expected, certainly for such a marginal and in some ways self-marginalised figure) muses about "Col S. J. Solomon" [Solomon J. Solomon] who is the head of camouflage operations and "whom I know a bit". He concludes: "I wonder if I'd be any good at it. Who would I have to approach about it. Do write". It is perhaps ironic that a portrait painter of distinction should have headed up the camouflage operations during the war. But the extraordinary situation – not least the relationships between the artists and the military – becomes clearer if one reads *Churchill's Wizards* by Nicholas Rankin which is at once an entertaining and scholarly account of British "deception" in the first and second world wars.

Solomon conducted experiments in his garden and, in all ways, took his responsibilities seriously. He was already promoting his ideas to senior officers while serving as a private in The Artists Rifles (this interesting connection needs to be confirmed – or not – when physical access to his service record, kept at Kew, becomes available) and visited the front lines in December 1915. He was commissioned as a temporary Lieutenant-Colonel in the Royal Engineers in January 1916 on the say-so of the commander of the British forces on the western Front, Sir Douglas Haig, presumably so that he would have authority to get things done as an equal with senior figures at the front. And indeed he met Haig there, as well as the French camouflage authorities and experts. This role lasted a few months. He worked with the French on designing trees that would camouflage observation posts. He rightly claimed that artists had a contribution to make to the war effort. The Cubists as well as the Futurists influenced the French military efforts in the territory of deception achieved by concealment. Aesthetic creation is not always so (potentially) useful on such a scale. Rankin notes that "Solomon had the artistic vision to point the way to the use of military camouflage, but he had no understanding of the human and military organisation required to achieve it". Leading artists who contributed to the invention and practice of camouflage techniques in World War One included Paul Klee, Franz Marc, Edward Wadsworth, Jacques Villon and Dunoyer de Segonzac.

Solomon's medal index card spells "both" his names wrong: Soloman. After or before receiving the Russian Order of Saint Anna (3rd class), which was gazetted on January 14, 1918, Solomon returned to England and became a technical advisor on the controversial issue of tank camouflage, setting up a camouflage school in Hyde Park (that part of it now known as Kensington Gardens) which, according to Wikipedia, was taken over by the army. His influence was most felt through his co-invention or simultaneous invention of camouflage fish netting, the most widely used screening of World War One. And it is as an inventor and technical master that he is now remembered. In 1919, the artist was commissioned by Sir Douglas Haig's alma mater, Clifton College, to paint Haig's portrait, four years before Polack's[4].

4. On the subject of commemoration: I have been associated with a committee which has been trying to organise a bust of Isaac Rosenberg that will grace a building associated with him or his work. At the time of writing the commission of a bronze has not been finalised. Originally, the sculptor Hannah Northam made a small study, a clay model. It is a beautiful and moving likeness based on the poet's self-portrait now in the National Portrait Gallery. See the cover of the present work.

14) ISAAC ROSENBERG AND COMPANY

The first list comprises writers who were also visual artists:

Hans Christian Andersen, Antonin Artaud, Elizabeth Bishop, William Blake, the Bronte sisters, Phillip Callow, Mario Cesarini, Jean Cocteau, Gunter Grass, Alasdair Gray, Victor Hugo, D. H. Lawrence, Edward Lear, Wyndham Lewis, Henri Michaux, Stanley Middleton, Flannery O'Connor, Mervyn Peake, Sylvia Plath, Isaac Rosenberg, Bruno Schultz, Adrian Stokes, August Strindberg, Giorgio Vasari.

The second list comprises visual artists who were or are also writers:

Arp, Bellmer, Cellini, Giacometti, Kandinsky, Kitaj, Klee, Pierre Klossowski, Magritte, Masson, Michelangelo, Picasso, Schwitters.[5]

5. Some readers might dispute the characterisations, especially those of Blake and Wyndham Lewis. Cellini wrote a great autobiography, and so on. I should mention Van Gogh: a special case, the author of the most profound written record of artistic creativity we have, in the shape of his letters. David Jones could be in both lists, as could Dante Gabriel Rossetti, and Miriam Neiger-Fleischmann, painter and poet and my co-translator of the poems of Avigdor Hameiri in the present work. Ezra Pound had a second string, as a composer, followed by Anthony Burgess and preceded by Jean-Jacques Rousseau. And then there are Posy Simmonds and Raymond Briggs and Art Spiegelman… Sophie Calle…

15) ISAAC ROSENBERG AND CARL RAKOSI

Carl Rakosi, who lived till he was over a hundred, was the sweetest and dearest man. Had he, the only American Objectivist poet born in Europe, been Charles Reznikoff's age (i.e. ten years older) or Isaac Rosenberg's age (thirteen years older), he would have been the right age to be my grandfather. I thought of him as an old uncle or a very young great-uncle. He was the wittiest and most provocative of the Objectivists, and would have had plenty to say to the Leeds Rosenberg centenary conference in 2018, as he did about a previous one on poetry and war (which I organised for the Cambridge Poetry Festival in 1981), when his message (see 'Rakosi' in the bibliography) arrived too late to be read out. It denounced the whole idea of the conference and began: "I do have a message for you symposiasts: get your heads out of that noose!…. [Carl's dots] the noose being the moral horse-collar which you put on when you enter the question, 'While Rome burns…. etc'. We went through all that in the GREAT DEPRESSION [his upper case]. Does each generation have to agonize over the same wrong questions?" Reznikoff wrote a novel about the Jews of York, *The Lionhearted*, a subject which would surely have engaged Isaac Rosenberg, had he survived the war.

16) ISAAC ROSENBERG AND GEOFFREY HILL AND CHRIS SEARLE

Although Chris Searle doesn't name him in his autobiography *Isaac and I*, his tutor, when he was a first year undergraduate at Leeds in 1963, can be identified as Geoffrey Hill. Searle found the tutorials "places of fear". However, more than fifty years later, in 2014, he came across Hill's *Collected Critical Writings* and turned to the essay on Rosenberg, which was "full of insight, passion and indignation," and then, Searle continues, Hill – "asked to find the most succinct description of Rosenberg's 'desire' – wrote: 'the desire to free his voice'. To free his voice from what? From the condition of being regarded, or disregarded, as an 'expendable young Hebrew', a slave in the vast pool of London labour ; subsequently, by single exception, as an unidentifiable waste item in Field Marshal Haig's ever-increasing expenditure of blood and treasure". Searle goes on to regret that Geoffrey Hill did not discuss Ben Jonson, Marvell and Donne in such a passionate way back in 1963, nor was Rosenberg present in his canon: "If only Isaac had been there then" Searle writes, what a connection Searle and Hill might have made, or so Searle imagines, sweetly but perhaps over-optimistically. Elizabeth Cook reckons that Rosenberg was already in Hill's canon, referring to his poem, 'For Isaac Rosenberg', published in *Isis* in 1952.

Searle went on to write a thesis on Rosenberg for McMaster University in Hamilton, Ontario, in which he argued that Rosenberg's poems had their precedent in the mythopoeic work of Blake, incarnating and heralding a rebellion against tyranny, and that he was not solely a lyric poet disgusted by war and empathising with its victims. Searle's later passionate involvement in politics and education was directly inspired by Rosenberg, including the two letters I cited earlier with their emphasis on "devastating" and "devastation". These letters have the kind of youthful authority we find in Rimbaud's 'Lettres du voyant' (admittedly Rosenberg was about ten years older than the 16 year old boy genius), and remind one of Czeslaw Milosz's phrase in

The Witness of Poetry, which I have quoted in other essays and books: "the pressure of history on experience".

Re-reading Hill's essay I cannot help connecting the phrase of Milosz to the following assertion: "His [Rosenberg's] forgetfulness [was] not actually a sign of weakness but of strength – the immense strength of other priorities, such as working on massive and complex poems in your head amid the manifold terrors and routine hard labour of life in the trenches". Which brings me to Charles Hobday.

17) ISAAC ROSENBERG AND CHARLES HOBDAY

Charles Hobday, poet and radical left-wing historian, claims that others, notably Isaac Rosenberg's three biographers, play down Rosenberg's left-wing politics. While Hobday's *London Magazine* article, 'Isaac Rosenberg: Revolutionary Poet' serves as a corroboration from the left field and possible corrective, he exaggerates when he says that cold-war pieties influenced the biographers. Furthermore, to suggest, admittedly with the powerful support of Edgell Rickword, that Rosenberg possibly self-censored his poems since, included in letters, they might be objected to by army censors, is unlikely in the extreme, if only because the great trench poems resist the reading that politicisation would a) be necessary and b), if necessary, be an improvement.

When the war began, says Hobday, Rosenberg was preoccupied by "art, social crisis and revolution". Reading with and against Hobday, I would summarise Rosenberg's politics as follows: like all his friends in the East End, he was a left-wing radical, partly inspired by one of the traditions in his ancestral religion which, in turn, was only one of the influences on a poor working class Jewish boy in that neighbourhood. Again, like his friends, the Whitechapel Boys, he was for a while a member of the Young Socialist League, a Marxist organisation and the youth wing of the Social Democratic Party. In his youth, he had been "socialist, then anarchist, and always anti-capitalist and so anti-militarist", as reported by his friend John Rodker. (Rosenberg attended the clubs of the great East End anarchist Rudolf Rocker at Toynbee Hall and in Jubilee Street. The Rosenberg family were living in Jubilee Street in 1906, when the club opened). But he was not a full-on ideological Marxist, nor was he a political Zionist in the later sense. The son of Tolstoyan pacifists, his Zionism, if the word applies at all, was a component of his religious heritage, a heritage he never disowned but which he ceased to practise in an orthodox way.

Another influence was the radical tradition in English poetry, including Blake, Byron and Shelley. Like Chagall later on, Rosenberg drew on Christian iconography as a Jewish dimension. Marxism, Judaism and Christianity, Hobday argues, were parallel influences, as indeed they were. Hobday believes that *Moses* owes more to Marxism than to Judaism. But in the play Rosenberg is saying that God needs to be re-invented. It is a classic case of the eternal Jewish agon with or against God. Most of Rosenberg's friends and family were anti-war and it is well known that he joined up for economic reasons; he exaggerated when he said he liked army life, doubtless because he was on the defensive. However he certainly did not lay the blame for the War solely on the Germans, as is clear from his letter to Trevelyan about the latter's play *The Pterodamozels*. [See section 21].

Hobday makes much of two poems 'Soldier, Twentieth Century' and 'Girl to a Soldier on Leave', which according to Noakes – and *pace* Hobday – may have been written in France not in England where he did not fear censorship. The soldiers on both sides, before revolutionary enlightenment, "slept like Circe's swine", passive victims of leaders like Napoleon, Caesar and – Rosenberg implies, according to Hobday – Haig, who may unintentionally awaken them and turn them, collectively, into potential leaders, mutineers, "Titans". "Babel cities' smoky tops" is a metonymy for industrialisation and the consequential exploitation of workers. The Russian Revolution has begun and there are mutinies in all the armies. The girl in the second poem feels guilt for not restraining the soldier more. Hobday says the ten days leave Isaac Rosenberg spent with his family reawakened his consciousness of his Jewish heritage. In fact, Rosenberg made a personal choice to seek and take leave during the ten days of penitence, from New Year to Yom Kippur [see below, section 18]. His consciousness of the heritage needed no reawakening. He alludes to this leave in a short letter to his father of October 1917, which begins: "I am glad you are satisfied with my Yomtov energy", Yomtov meaning festival. Elkon, Isaac's brother, was also home on leave.

18) ISAAC ROSENBERG AND A.C. JACOBS

In his poem, 'In Early Spring', one of Rosenberg's successors, A. C. Jacobs (see *Nameless Country*, selected poems edited by Merle Bachman and myself), summons up his own verses and then provides the names of his poetic ancestors: Yehuda Halevi, Moses Ibn-Ezra, Bialik, Heine, the Yiddish poets, "And tragic Rosenberg whom a war killed / Before he could get his great things into words; / My friend Jon Silkin…". The remark about Rosenberg rightly takes him at his own estimation concerning future work, in that the poet quite naturally had a different perspective about his written and unwritten poems than we do, but it is a touch hyperbolic for Jacobs must have been aware that Isaac Rosenberg *did* get some great things into words. Rosenberg might have known that in Hebrew "davar" means both word and thing.

19) ISAAC ROSENBERG: JEWISH POET

The only leave Rosenberg was permitted during his entire time in France coincided in September 1917 with the ten days of penitence, the Jewish high holidays, beginning with the New Year and ending with Yom Kippur. This cannot be a coincidence. Subject to military priorities, the army did make it possible for leave to be offered to Jewish soldiers and sailors during this period. In earlier correspondence with his parents, Rosenberg discusses possible leave for Passover, so it is likely that they encouraged the timing and that it would also have been his own choice.

In the first of his poems to survive, 'Ode to David's Harp', the fifteen-year old Rosenberg seeks to "wake the zeal in Israel's breast". Charles Tomlinson, in his valuable pamphlet, *Isaac Rosenberg of Bristol*, rightly refers to Rosenberg as a religious poet, though he could have been more explicit. Rosenberg is, among other things, a specifically *Jewish* religious poet (touched on more in Tomlinson's article on the plays, which I discuss later in this section), although not a practising orthodox Jew. Tomlinson also emphasises Rosenberg's regular use of the word "hear", so central to the Jewish liturgy and practice which were part of his life. As mentioned already in the brief discussion about Jon Silkin, Rosenberg's Jewishness is central to his poetry and plays. One could speculate that drama, verse drama, would have engaged him later as much as poetry, because of the inherently dramatic, often agonistic, relationship between Jewish believers (belief imprinted on his psyche and in his work thanks to his early upbringing) and God; the influence of Shakespeare and Milton and Blake are there in his play *Moses*, written with deep personal involvement as well as saturation in English literature and its partial roots in the Bible, the King James Version being a foundational classic of the literature. ("Roots": a crucial word for Rosenberg who would have known Blake's phrase, "struggle of entanglement with incoherent roots").

According to Christopher Ricks and Jim McCue, T.S. Eliot

considered writing a preface for a new edition of Rosenberg's poems in 1935 but was dissuaded. Eliot, an exact contemporary, had long been an admirer of Rosenberg's war poetry ("the most remarkable of the poets killed in that war") and in a 'Commentary' in July 1935 in *The Criterion*, wrote: "It is not a matter of indifference that poetry written by an Irishman, a Welshman, a Scot, an American or a Jew should be undistinguishable from that written by an Englishman: it is undesirable. The poetry of Isaac Rosenberg, for instance, does not only owe its distinction to its being Hebraic: but *because* it is Hebraic it is a contribution to English literature. For a Jewish poet to be able to write like a Jew, in Western Europe and in a western European language, is almost a miracle; and for different reasons and in different degrees it is also difficult for the other people I have mentioned". The curious implication in this complicated compliment to the author of "Hebraic" poetry is that Jewish poets are assumed or supposed to write in Hebrew. However, this is a side-issue.

Plays that Rosenberg might have written would have challenged T. S. Eliot to do better, or at least differently. Geoffrey Hill states – in an essay about F. T. Prince which I commissioned for a special issue of *PNR* –that Eliot's failure to complete the Coriolan sequence "was a tragic failure". By now Rosenberg would have made decisions about the use of blank verse and free verse, both of which he had already mastered, as vehicles for drama. Rosenberg's post-WW1 and pre-WW2 poems might have impacted on Eliot (and vice versa), fatefully influencing his previous views on Jews, and perhaps his prosody too. Faced with such a challenge, *Four Quartets* would have read very differently.

Did Eliot ever reflect on how one might read the rat in one of his lesser poems, 'Burbank with a Baedecker', in the light of Rosenberg's "queer, sardonic rat…..droll rat" with its "cosmopolitan sympathies" (including German soldiers) in 'Break of Day in the Trenches'? Thanks to Ezra Pound, 'Break of Day…' was published in *Poetry Chicago* in December 1916, where Eliot would certainly have read it. 'Burbank with a Baedecker' was published in *Art and Letters* in Summer, 1919. Too late for Rosenberg, although 'Prufrock' was not, since it was first published in *Poetry Chicago* in June 1915, thanks again to Pound. You might say that Eliot's sensibility was dissociated or you might take care to dissociate Eliot's private views from the story in a poem, depending on your critical standpoint. (To discuss over a drink in some estaminet). Later, Rosenberg might also have influenced and found favour with the 'New Apocalypse' poets of the 1940s, now the subject of a welcome and belated major anthology *Apocalypse*, edited by James Keery.

The whole question of slavery and freedom and the Exodus from Egypt as explored in *Moses* is central to Jewish self-understanding and indeed self-existence, and influences those who are no longer religious as well as other religions and cultures, as evidenced by American slave songs. It would strongly affect Rosenberg's thoughts about being a private soldier in the trenches, not least as a Jewish private. Peter Lawson in his book *Anglo-Jewish Poetry from Isaac Rosenberg to Elaine Feinstein*, explores the way Rosenberg's vision of Zion faces the future, Siegfried Sassoon's the past. Rosenberg's profoundly Jewish and profoundly personal agon with the Jewish God – the God not only of the Exodus but also the *Akeda*, the Binding of Isaac (a major theme in Deborah Maccoby's monograph on Rosenberg, *God Made Blind*) – would surely have paralleled his spiritual vision of Zion, had he survived. Note should be made of his heterodox invocations of Adam's first wife Lilith and her virtual opposite, the *Shekhina*, the female principle of God, and a central feature of Jewish esoteric literature.

Charles Tomlinson, in an important article on the plays, especially *Moses*, refers to the "syntactic entanglement" resulting from the "pressure at which Rosenberg allows thoughts and words to interact and [which] is justified by its expressive completeness". When Moses elaborates the hope of harmony, a new order, it involves "the night-side of being, the suppressed half of which floods in to give us the immediate intuition of a new fullness". And it involves music. "The equation sought for (to venture an abstract and inadequate formula) is one in which desire, hope, beauty and fate stand on the one side and music on the other, and Rosenberg's development was bound up with finding the right poetic means to convince us that this equation can be true."

Nubian: Beauty is a great paradox –
Music's secret soul, creeping about the senses
To wrestle with man's coarser nature.
It is hard when beauty loses.

Lilith: I think beauty is a bad bargain made of life.

(from *The Amulet*)

There will be, in Rosenberg's words, "a consciousness / Like naked light seizing the all-eyed soul". The powers and energy found in Moses ("from whose loins I sprung", writes Rosenberg in 'The Jew' of 1915 or 1916, written after his miserable experience during post-enlistment training, when he experienced anti-semitism, see letter to Schiff of October, 1915), will be expressed more fully and also more sparely in his great poems, for which he was preparing all along. As Tomlinson says, "From the beginning, Rosenberg realised with the certainty of genius, the questions that he was called upon, that he was *fated* to answer in his poetry." Another post-war connection that could not take place would have been Rosenberg and Gurney, when the talk would undoubtedly have turned to music.

20) ISAAC ROSENBERG'S READING MATTER[6]

On August 19, 1916, Isaac Rosenberg writes to Gordon Bottomley to tell him that he has received "the Georgian book" [*Georgian Poetry 1913–1915*, edited by Edward Marsh], "but it is so awkward out here to have books in cloth that I must send it back again." Around the same time, he wrote the weak patriotic poem 'Pozières', which he submitted the following year with a drawing for the 40th Division's Christmas card. It was, unsurprisingly to us, and perhaps to him too, rejected. Anthony Powell wrongly states in a review in the *Daily Telegraph* in 1975 that Rosenberg designed the eventual card.

In a letter to Sidney Schiff of August or September 1916, Rosenberg makes the same point he made to Bottomley: "Thank you for Lawrence offer but cloth books are so bulky and impossible out here". However, a letter to Marsh in August provides evidence that Rosenberg read *Georgian Poetry* before sending it back, because he says that Rupert Brooke's poem on "Clouds" is magnificent. Perhaps Rosenberg is praising Brooke

6. In 1939 Sir Herbert Read published his anthology *The Knapsack* for the use of soldiers with little space for books in their kit. He tells us that his own constant companion in World War One was Robert Bridges' anthology, *The Spirit of Man*. David Jones took two books when he went to war: Palgrave's *Golden Treasury* and an unknown title. Wouldn't we love to know what it was! Robert Graves took Blake, Leavis took Milton, Edgell Rickword took Grierson's recently published edition of Donne, Ernst Junger took *Tristram Shandy*. In World War Two, the poet Bernard Spencer took little books of paintings by Masaccio, Fra Angelico and Giotto. General Eisenhower's bedside book, unexpectedly, was Thomas Carlyle's *Sartor Resartus*.

Robert Graves published a substantial essay on Rosenberg in 1927 (Graves and Riding: A Survey of Modernist Poetry, 1927), while Leavis in New Bearings in English Poetry (1932) reserved special praise for and appreciation of Rosenberg. Both were survivors of the western front, Leavis as a member of the Friends Ambulance Unit, Graves as an officer in the Welsh Guards, his service so brilliantly evoked in Goodbye to All That.

so highly because he knows that Marsh rates Brooke as a poet far more seriously than he himself does: Brooke's poems "remind me too much of flag-days", he wrote in another letter to Sidney Schiff in the summer of 1916. Rosenberg, significantly, took with him to the front the poems of John Donne – as did many other poets – a fact which John Lucas reckons could merit an article in its own right. He also took Thomas Browne's *Religio Medici*.

Many commentators have drawn attention to Rosenberg's reading of the great English poet during the war, not least his three main biographers. It was Winifreda Seaton, a school teacher, who introduced Rosenberg to Donne around 1910. This influence took the years of the war to make itself more fully felt or thought, for in his letter to Seaton (written in London between October 1913 and January 1914), he expresses a preference for Francis Thompson's 'Dream Tryst' over Donne's 'The Ecstasy', and says that Verhaern (sic)" knocks Donne into a cocked hat. I mean for genuine poetry". A great deal of Donne "seems a sort of mental gymnastics". Later references to Donne are more respectful: Donne was "chokeful of meaningful ideas". In a later letter to Seaton, written from hospital in France (15 November 1917), Rosenberg comments that "nearly all our big poets" (Shakespeare, Donne, Keats, Milton, Blake) did most of their work in London. Three of the big poets, Donne, Blake and Keats, are among his major avatars.

In an undated letter to his father, received on August 11, 1917, Rosenberg says that the aforementioned "Mrs Herbert Cohen sent me a little book compiled by the Chief Rabbi of Jewish interest". This was the anthology *A Book of Jewish Thoughts* edited by Chief Rabbi Joseph Hertz, which was indeed first published in 1917 and sent to many if not all Jewish soldiers and sailors during the remainder of World War One and also throughout World War Two. It was reprinted as a "library edition" in 1920, which I possess. It's still easy to buy or read online. Hertz lived until 1946. Perhaps a revised edition for World War Two was not considered necessary. It won't be required in World War Three.

21) ISAAC ROSENBERG AND AVIGDOR HAMEIRI

Born in 1886 (Wikipedia says 1890, which is wrong according to a leading authority, Miriam Neiger-Fleischmann), the Hungarian Hebrew poet and novelist Avigdor Hameiri wrote short stories and volumes of poetry about his experience as a soldier and prisoner of war in World War One. He also wrote two extraordinary and neglected expressionistic and non-militaristic if not actually pacifist memoirs or rather documentary novels or auto-fiction: *The Great Madness* and *Hell on Earth*, which anticipate later literature of the Holocaust and World War Two – such as the novels of Piotr Rawicz and Ka-Tsetnik 135633 – and which Hameiri also wrote about in novels like *The White Messiah*. More widely read in Hebrew than *All Quiet on the Western Front*, *The Great Madness* was the first Hebrew best-seller in pre-State Israel. Published in 1929, it contains two poems that belong in the present essay, along with a third and later poem. 'Blood Rose' and 'Without Eulogies' were published in Hebrew magazines in Odessa just after the war. They belong in three worlds, that of German and European expressionist poetry, that of the war poetry of Isaac Rosenberg and others on both sides, and the bible-influenced Hebrew poetry and culture Hameiri absorbed as a traditionally educated Hungarian Jew involved in literary activities beyond religious *yeshiva* studies.

Sadly, perhaps shamefully, my Hebrew is not up to reading Hameiri's poetry with full understanding in the original. I am dependent on Miriam Neiger-Fleischmann for interpretation and co-translation. Hameiri wrote about fifty poems of war. On the strength of the three published here and on his two translated novels, he belongs among the important writers of war and, as a Hebrew writer, unique as a chronicler of World War One. Rosenberg would have recognised this, just as Hameiri would have recognised the quality, power and significance of Rosenberg's work, had he lived long enough to read the poems in Hebrew translation. Hameiri lived until 1980 and in the sixty years following World War One, published many volumes of poetry, short stories, novels and essays, and became one of the major Hebrew writers of the twentieth century. His life and work supply a tantalising glimpse of what Rosenberg might have become, had he lived as long as his almost exact contemporary.

Hameiri served on the Russian front until he was captured. He left for the Yishuv (pre-state Jewish community in British Mandate Palestine) in 1921. His progressive politics were opposite to those of Uri Zvi Greenberg's and closer to Rosenberg's. What's more, the English poet's Jewishness was not that of Greenberg, for whom the fact that Jews fought on both sides (and that he ended up in captivity in Russia) involved big issues and led to radical right-wing Zionism. There is no doubt that Rosenberg would have written a prose memoir of some kind, perhaps a reckoning, with the officer class in the dock (see section 21). Surely Rosenberg and Hameiri would have become friends and compared many notes. Rosenberg would also have engaged with Greenberg. It is interesting to note that Hameiri and Greenberg were respectful of each other and remained friends throughout their lives. These poems by Hameiri were co-translated by Miriam Neiger-Fleischmann and myself.

BLOODY ROSE

Wherever we may be, it makes no difference,
Every kiss is fruitful, every colour bloody.
Come to my grave, let's make love once more.

Don't be frightened, it's only me you'll find there,
Your warm flesh will lie upon my patch of soil
And my fresh blood will perfume your harvest.

Our sacred orgasm is rooted in this earth.
Come kiss me with horror for the last time.
Let our Creator look down and rejoice in his handiwork.

And let the creatures who pick in graves observe
And understand the holy passions of the flesh
And they will be gently blessed and fertile

And then we will be reunited, forever.
You, bloody rose, you will blossom on my grave
And your colour will radiate from my sap.

WITHOUT EULOGY AND SHROUD

Thousands go crazy around me
And my mind remembers it all.
In a moment, my time will come,
Unnoticed by everybody.

Zhazhazha. How lovely is the song of death,
My heart chokes in my throat.
Zhazhazha. Oh grandfather, oh mother.
Oh my Lord, oh my God.

My scalp sweats out a deadly toxin.
Zhazhazha. Close your eyes quickly.
Impure ravens will soon
Be feasting on me

And your fresh heart will be torn to pieces,
I will be rotten under the bushes.
Zhazha. Get rid of me quickly.
Without a shroud, without a eulogy.

SATAN'S IDYLL

The town square is the goddam cemetery,
Accursèd silence in the pit.
The woodlark circles overhead
(Its stomach filled with human flesh).
Here be miracles in the spring light.

The sun spreads in all its glory,
The channels of its splendour split apart,
Flower makes love to flower,
(Blood, love's sap, intoxicates us).
Make love to me. Kiss me more.

All around, the dead, rotting,
Stinking and decaying in the heat
And the earth of the battle-field sleeps,
(Hoary offspring of a whore)
Digests the corpses while it dreams.

And a bee drops slowly from above
On a flower dirtied by blood –
How weird, thinks the bee. Buzz buzz.
(Oh stubborn presence of the *Shekhina*).
The bee sucks the nauseous blood.

The Hebrew word for 'woodlark' is *khugah*. Hameiri's human-flesh eating lark is a far cry (or trill) from the cheerfully violent French song we used to sing at school about a flesh-eaten lark: "Alouette, gentille alouette"… in which everything is plucked. According to Miriam Neiger-Fleischmann (private communication), Hameiri would have known Felix Mendelsohn's 'Song of the Lark'. She says it is certain he would have known the Hebrew translation (it was entitled 'Hakhugah', 'The wood-lark'), published in Odessa for Hebrew schools in 1903. I cannot resist wondering if Isaac Babel, who was born in Odessa nine years later and lived there for most of his childhood and knew Hebrew, read this poem.

Later, in a 1940 poem about the London Blitz, 'Prothalamion' (in *Wedding Poems*), quoted in full by John Matthias and also by James Keery in the major new anthology *Apocalypse* which I have already mentioned, David Jones concludes with his own war:

So I have heard bird-song,
        Beneath the

Trajectory zone, at Passchendaele, or seen
Flowers lean towards each other under the sun
That shined to delineate the hate and mutilation
Of the Forward Area

The Keery volume contains at least one other World War Two poem explicitly referencing World War One, the matrix war, such as Edmund Blunden's 'Exorcised' and a post-World War Two poem by Robert Graves: 'Surgical Ward: Men'. Had Rosenberg survived he would have certainly been included in this important book, which completely changes the way we read post-World War Two poetry.

Post-script: Hameiri enters a poem by the major Yiddish poet Avraham Sutzkever, who met the older poet in Omsk, Siberia , in 1917, when Hameiri was a prisoner of war and Sutzkever was a young boy. I translated this poem with Miriam Neiger-Fleischmann, from the Hebrew translation by Mordechai Sverdlik. One can easily imagine Rosenberg's parents making the same blessings on the eve of the Sabbath. The encounter with Hameiri, according to Neiger-Fleischmann's unpublished paper on the encounter given at a conference in Moscow in 2019, played a great part in Sutzkever's[7] becoming a poet.

ONCE IN WINTER

(Memento to Avigdor Hameiri)

That Sabbath eve we had no candles in our house,
over wet sticks mother made the *Shabbos* blessing.
A demon froze the light above us in his icy mouth
and father was lying on the straw, dark as a smoke stain.

7. http://www.moreshet.org/?CategoryID=199&ArticleID=468. If you right-click onto the menu and select "English translation", you can find Sutzkever's obituary of the leader of the Vilna Ghetto, the poet Abba Kovner. The connections between Greenberg, Hameiri, Sutzkever and Kovner are of great interest in terms of poetry and politics, and would have enthralled Rosenberg.

The deer, our neighbour, turned the glass to silver with its antlers
and the Siberian wind blew into our father's head.
My wise father made the *Kiddush* from his bed
but the wine cup was dripping while his arm quivered.

That Sabbath eve a shadow hovered over the *challo* loaves
which were not sliced by knife but by my poor mother's tears.
Then suddenly a young guest with heavy boots entered the house,
frost dropping off his fur coat as if shaken from a tree.

Jewish prisoner of war, Hungarian infantry survivor…
lieutenant from Franz Joseph's army… Hebrew writer.
His gaze was like **a** gazelle's: terrified and bitter…
and at once he gently lifted me on his shoulder

and he was no longer a guest but belonged to our family.
Sitting relaxed, alas he fell into gloom and longing –
father and mother, Sabbath and me, and our dwelling,
we all shared the beat of his biblical songs.

My silhouette rises like a scale. Upon it and around us,
delighted, perfumed, warm tunes were climbing tiptoe
and an almond tree in blossom appeared in the frozen glass
depicted by the heavy booted soldier – our poet.

Now I came to see *him* – at the doorstep I met an old timer.
The green window reflected the almond blossom,
and the poet returned to that time, my home, songs remembered,
a life story from long ago was floating once more in the air.

His eyes were like a gazelle's again: resisting but this time not scared,
We spoke with longing about that wintry Sabbath in Siberia.

22) ISAAC ROSENBERG AND HIS POSSIBLE FUTURES

There is every reason to suppose Rosenberg would have remained radical; this son of "Tolstoyans" would surely have found a home in a left-wing group, perhaps on its margins. Rosenberg sometimes mentions pathways concerning future work, presumably thinking of the eventual post-war period: "The doctor here too, Major Devoral, is a ridiculous bullying brute and I have marked him for special treatment when I come to write about the army" (Letter to Schiff, early December 1915). It feels as though this would have been a frontal attack in prose, possibly satirical, rather than verse or drama. What we have lost.

On the question of futures, one has to consider Rosenberg's state of mind, and also think about the crack-up and fate of Ivor Gurney, as well as about the fragility of David Jones, who recovered from a break-down but recovered, while remaining fragile. Rosenberg did not have Gurney's history of mental illness, which ante-dated the war, and he was tougher than his two fellow poets. But, even if he had survived the episode which killed him on April 1, 1918, there were still six months of the war to go. And in a letter postmarked 16 January 1918, he had written the following to Marsh, which I have used as an epigraph to this book: "What is happening to me now is more tragic than the 'passion play'. Christ never endured what I endure. It is breaking me completely". These two sentences were censored.

So, one mind game is to wonder what Isaac Rosenberg would have written had he survived the war. Another, proposed by Alan Wall, is to wonder what the poet would have written had there been no war. However, the greatest wonder is that he wrote any poems at all, let alone great ones, in the circumstances of trench warfare. "Mad Ireland hurt you into poetry", wrote Auden of Yeats. Perhaps it is futile to give this idea the time of day, *mutatis mutandis*, when it comes to Rosenberg, even if Auden means that Yeats was hurt into a different kind of poetry than he would otherwise have written. Rosenberg prepared himself in the

Whitechapel Library and at all times, antennae on full alert, to write serious poetry, exploring the deeps in heightened language. If it had not been the war, something else would have lit the fuse.

I have already discussed the attraction verse plays held for him. The fragments we have suggest he might have joined Eliot and forgotten figures from the next generation, Christopher Fry, Ronald Duncan and Jonathan Griffin, as poets writing for the theatre, the latter's poetry possibly influenced by Gurney's. I cherish the thought that my friend Griffin's verse play *The Hidden King* would have been in dialogue with works by the older Rosenberg. Rosenberg's older friend and supporter Gordon Bottomley wrote a verse drama, *King Lear's Wife*, referred to in the letter to Ruth Löwy and published in the Georgian anthology sent to Rosenberg. While home on leave in 1917, Rosenberg read the satirical verse play *The Pterodamozels*, by another older friend, Robert Trevelyan, a text which appealed to his radical side. September 26, 1917: "The play is gorgeous, one of the chiefest pleasures of my leave days" but with an apparent reservation: "I only wish the thing had the power of its purpose". On October 18, back in France and in hospital with severe influenza, he writes: "I brought your play back with me but it's lost….. Your play was all I read at home". In a letter to Bottomley postmarked July 23 1916, Rosenberg had written: "Simple *poetry*, that is where an interesting complexity of thought is kept in tone and right value to the dominating idea so that it is understandable and still ungraspable. I know it is beyond my reach now, except in bits". Simple is an odd word in this context, unless it means "simply". It strikes me that his thought in this sentence makes good sense in the context of his existing plays and the plays he would never write. By the date he wrote the letter he had completed *Moses* and some of his significant poems including 'Break of Day in the Trenches', but not yet 'Dead Man's Dump'. Geoffrey Hill, in his essay, argues that "for the sake of advancing the idea" Rosenberg was, like Emerson, prepared to sacrifice "finality of phrase".

Another radical poet who survived World War One was Edgell Rickword whom I met when he was working as a bookseller in Charing Cross Road in the 1970s and corresponded with about his book on Rimbaud and other issues. Rickword's most famous poem, 'To the Wife of a Non-Interventionist Statesman' would have aroused Rosenberg's interest and they would surely have been in political dialogue about the world wars and of course about Spain. Rickword's handful of war poems were mostly written soon after the war, including the powerful 'Trench Poets'. It begins flatly: "I knew a man, he was my chum"'. Rickword is reading Donne and Tennyson to him, in a futile attempt to keep him alive. It ends: "He stank so badly, though we were great chums / I had to leave him; then rats ate his thumbs". These rats were neither droll nor cosmopolitan.

23) ISAAC ROSENBERG, KAFKA AND SAMUEL HUGO BERGMAN

Thanks to a London friend the late Rabbi Albert Friedlander, I met Samuel Hugo Bergman, philosopher and retired rector of the Hebrew University, on a visit to Jerusalem, in 1969. In his private study, he presented me with a copy of his introduction to modern Jewish thought, *Faith and Reason*, and inscribed it in Hebrew. Then the unforgettable moment: he allowed me to clasp the high-school-keepsake album of 1901 in which his classmate Franz Kafka (not yet our Kafka of course, and so all the more moving) had written a message.

The fantasy of meeting Kafka or, say, Isaac Rosenberg is, of course, different from the fantasy of meeting someone from earlier times, Flaubert or Dostoevsky or Rimbaud, none of whom one could have met. My friend the late Clive Sinclair did meet, and I corresponded with, one of Kafka's Hebrew teachers, Jerusalem-born Puah Ben-Tovim. Kafka encountered her while she was studying in Prague, introduced by their mutual friend, Hugo Bergman. To ruminate on meeting Kafka, one has to engage in one's own fantasy, just as Nicole Kraus did in her novel *Forest Dark*.

Let's pretend that Kafka was not a sick man and did not die aged forty in 1924 and that World War Two – in which he might have endured the same fate as his sisters but he might, too, have come to London with Dora Diamant – did not take place. He might have emigrated to Palestine – as he had said he might – and one would have sought him out on that visit in 1969, when he would have been eighty six, in Jerusalem or more likely Tel-Aviv. But had Kafka's health been good, he would have had a different psyche-soma and he would not have been the man and written the books that make one want to have met him in the first place, and which are the reason why I felt that frisson of *proximity-in-distance* when I held the high-school-keepsake book in Bergman's house. And had Rosenberg emigrated to Palestine, how long would he have lasted? One suspects he would have returned to Europe.

Long ago I wrote or thought that Rosenberg, in a letter, had raised the possibility of emigrating. But I checked the correspondence and consulted experts like Jean Moorcroft Wilson and Deborah Maccoby and Jean Liddiard, and I'm wrong. Even so, had he gone (perhaps with Bomberg as I suggested earlier), he might have stayed there. Away from England, he would have remained the lost grand-father of Anglo-Jewish poets, which is what he was anyway, and still accessible by post or in person. It was quite something to meet Isaac's younger brother David Burton in 1974, at the National Book League, when the poet himself would have been eighty-four. In 2019, following an email correspondence, I met Isaac's surviving nephew, Bernard Wynick, for the first time. He was accompanied by Rosenberg's fellow literary executor of Isaac, the poet's first cousin twice removed (and twice over, because the fathers of her grandparents were two of the brothers of Isaac), Shelley Swade, who is a retired GP. It was moving for me to talk shop with family members. I learned about younger members of the family, such as Shelley's son, the renaissance scholar Micha Lazarus of Trinity College Cambridge and the Warburg Institute, who have personal interest in their illustrious relative.

Rosenberg might have got to the Middle East during the war had he succeeded in his attempt to be transferred to the Jewish Battalion, which was then stationed in what would become Iraq – the warm climate would have suited his health better. But Jean Liddiard rightly speculates that religious or ancestral motivation could have played its part in his wish, so perhaps that was what I was thinking of. His final letter, dated March 28 and postmarked April 2, the day after he died, is to Edward Marsh. He encloses 'Through these Pale Cold Days' (his final poem) and says he wants to write a battle song for the Judeans, which appears to refer to the battalion, though it is difficult not to read it as referring to the Jewish inhabitants of Mandate Palestine. Among the volunteers for the Jewish Legion was Jacob Epstein. Epstein surely knew Donatello's *Binding of Isaac.* I wish he had made a version himself, to accompany *Jacob and the Angel.* What a dialogue Isaac and Jacob would have had, as they recalled their meetings in

Whitechapel and at the Café Royal, and Isaac's miraculous survival.

> We are lifted of all we know
> And hang from implacable boughs.

Name.	Corps.	Rank.	Regtl. No.
SOLOMAN.	R. Eo.	* Lt.-Col.	

SOLOMAN. JOSEPH.

Medal.	Roll.	Page.	Remarks.
VICTORY *	R.E. off. 144	9A	I.V. 5571/W.d.f. 16921 NW/8/3010
BRITISH	do	do	
STAR			

Theatre of War first served in

Date of entry therein

S.O. 1357 Escl. 9 16 NW/8/3010.

K. 1380.

Correspondence.

Address. 18 Hyde Pk Gate. S.W.

(35464—14a) Wt. W 3347—H.P 6451 2000m. 10/19 H. St Est. 6450/1250

Above: Solomon J. Solomon army index card

Above: John Parr memorial plaque at 52 Lodge Lane, London N12, close to where I live

Above: Self-portrait with helmet (Ben-Uri Collection)

Above: Linocut by Peter Paul Piech

Above: Linocut by Peter Paul Piech (in author's possession)

Above: Gas Warfare, from a suite of 22 lithographs by Gyula Zilzer (1932)

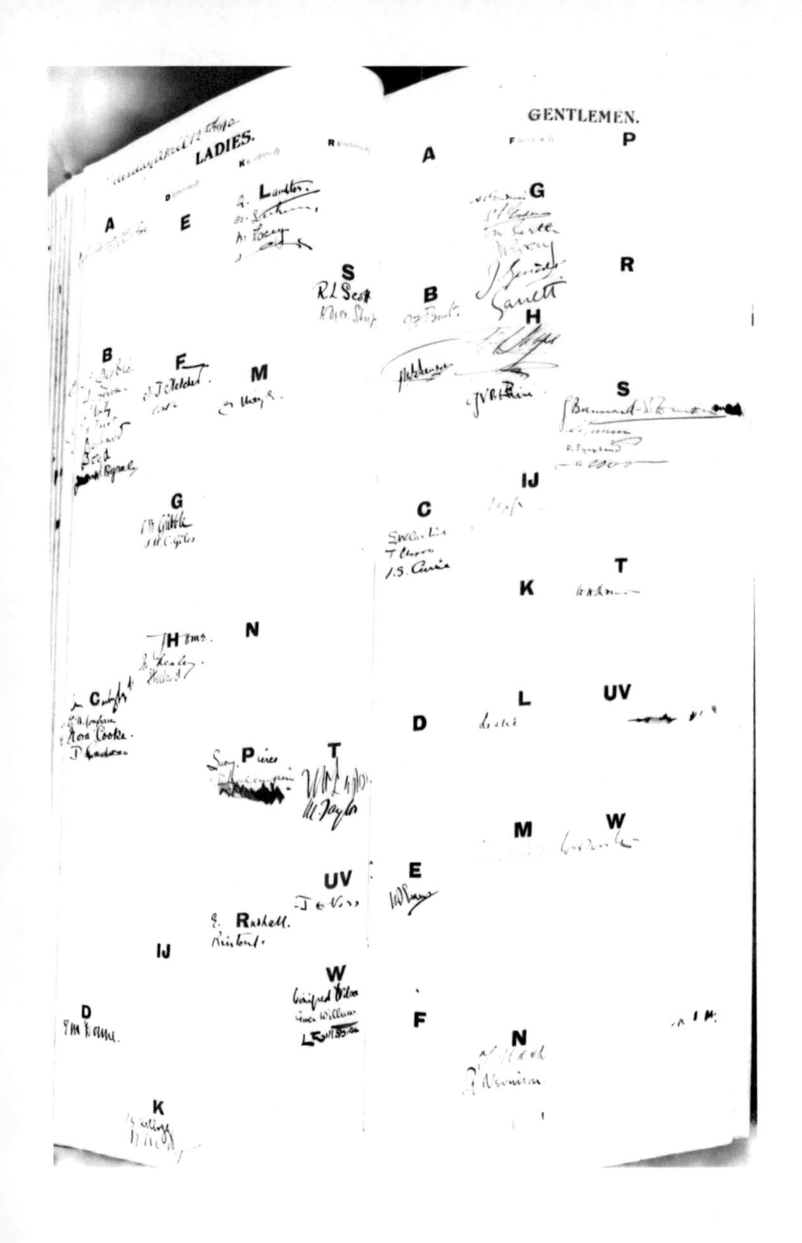

Above: Gilbert Bernard Solomon signature, Slade Signing in Book, April 1910.

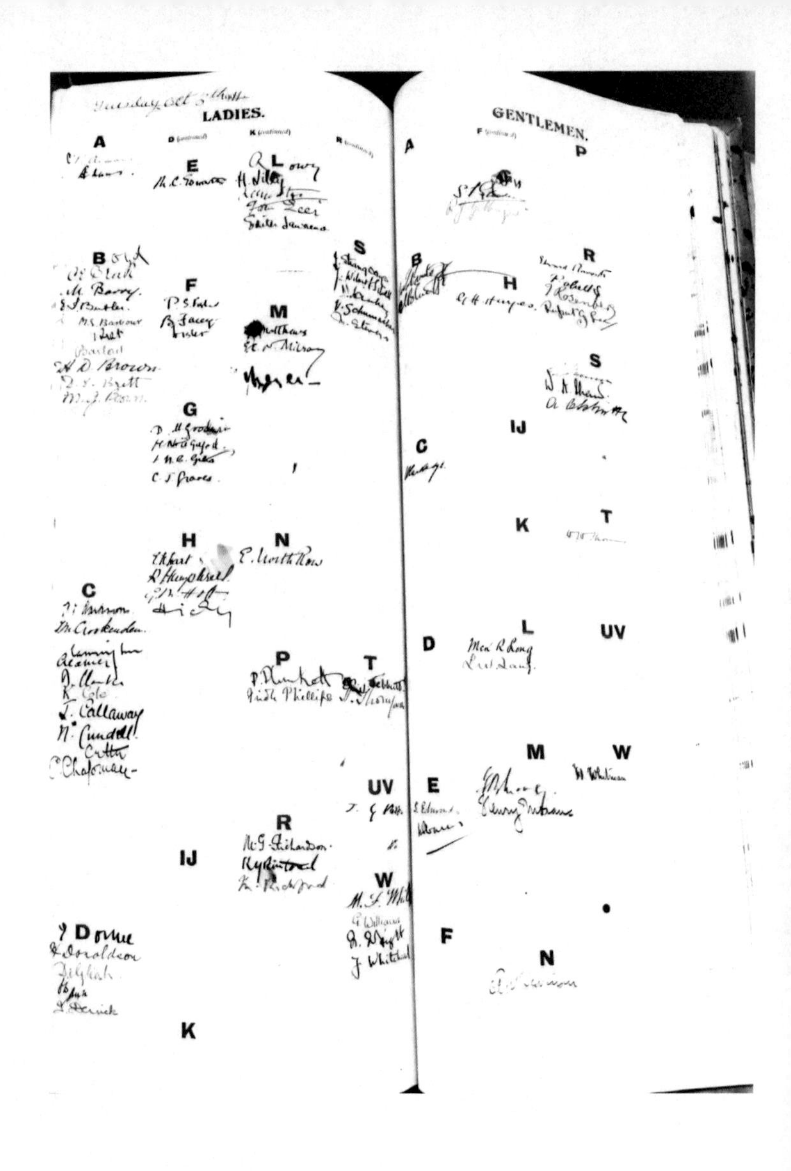

Above: Isaac Rosenberg signature, October 1911, Slade Signing In Book, Vol 16, 1909–1911

1st

F
20-21

1633.

RE-ENTRY FORM.

Form to be filled up by Students who are not Matriculated Students of the University and are re-entering the College.

UNIVERSITY OF LONDON.

UNIVERSITY COLLEGE.

Name in full Isaac Rosenberg

Address while attending the College 159 Oxford Street Mile End E

Home Address (if not as above)

Date of Birth 25th November 1890

Public Examination (if any) passed since the commencement of the preceding Session:

National Book Prize

Next Public Examination (if any) in view

Name and Address of Parent or Guardian (The person named here undertakes to be responsible for the payment of College dues) Guardian Mrs Cohen 2 Orme Court Kensington

Proposed Course of Study in the Faculty of Art

SUBJECTS.	Description of Class. Quote Index Letter.	
Drawing from life. Full time		

Union Society. Included in Composition Fee / Ordinary Subscription

Date 13 10 1911

Approved by the Faculty

Amount of Fees and Date of Payment 13.10

Above: Isaac Rosenberg

This book is a record of those members of University College London & of University College Hospital and Medical School who were killed or who died on service: 1914-1919

Volume II: Lister to Wynne

1924

Left and below: Roll of Honour – Rosenberg

ISAAC ROSENBERG was born in Bristol on November 25th, 1890, and came to London with his parents when he was seven. He was educated at the Board School of St. George's-in-the-East and at the Stepney Board School, where he showed so much promise in drawing and writing that the Headmaster allowed him to spend all his time practising them. At fourteen he was apprenticed to the firm of Carl Hentschel, and consoled himself for uncongenial work by writing poems in his meal-times, and attending classes at the Art School of Birkbeck College, where he won many prizes. In October, 1911, he entered the Slade School, and remained there until March, 1914. But "his true vocation was poetry," writes Mr. Laurence Binyon, "and he thought of himself as a poet rather than as a painter." His first pamphlet, "Night and Day," published in 1912, contains much of his early verse.

After leaving the Slade, Rosenberg sailed for Cape Town for the sake of his health. He returned in 1915 and enlisted in a "Bantam" Regiment, being subsequently drafted into the King's Own Royal Lancaster Regiment. He went out to France early in 1916, and was killed in action on April 1st, 1918. He was buried East of Arras, about one mile N.E. of Fampoux.

Rosenberg's verse has been collected and edited by Mr. Gordon Bottomley, with a memoir by Mr. Laurence Binyon (William Heinemann).

(Poems of Isaac Rosenberg; College Records; Photograph by permission of Mr. William Heinemann.)

ISAAC ROSENBERG

ROSENBERG Isaac 1633

Date of birth 25.11.1890

E.1911-12
L.1913-14
(March)

P) Ernest Lesser
13 Holland Villas Road.
Kensington

T) 1 St. George's Square,
Chalk Farm.

KILLED IN ACTION
1914-1918
DECEASED

SOLOMON, Gilbert Bernard

B.2.12.90

Ent. 1907-8

(P) B.S.Esq., 58 Priory Road, W.Hampstead.

(from U.S.)

Deceased
5/8/54

T.28.5.59.

Above: Rosenberg and Gilbert Solomon index cards

Over: Gilbert Bernard Solomon

Goodall Scholar

FIRST ENTRY FORM.

Form to be filled up by Non Matriculated Students of the University wishing to enter 1905 the College.

UNIVERSITY OF LONDON.

UNIVERSITY COLLEGE.

Name in full: Gilbert Bernard Solomon

Address while attending the College: 86 Priory Rd W Hampstead

Home Address (if not as above): —

Date of Birth: 8 December 2 1890

Previous place of education: University College School

Scholarship or Exhibition tenable at College: Goodall Ex:

~~Date of University Matriculation~~

Last Public Examination passed (if any) and date

Next Public Examination in view (if any) and date

Name and Address of Parent or Guardian (The person named here undertakes to be responsible for the payment of College dues): Bernard Solomon, 86 Priory Rd, W Hampstead

Proposed Course of Study in the Faculty of ~~Fine~~ Arts

SUBJECTS.	Description of Class. Quote Index Letter.	
Fine Arts 3rd Term	6 days	

Union Society. { Included in Composition Fee / Ordinary Subscription

Declaration of Adhesion to Regulations.

I, the undersigned, do hereby engage that I will conform to such regulations as have been, or may be, made for the maintenance of order in the College and in the Classes which I attend.

Date June 2nd 190

(Signed) G. B. Solomon

Approved by the Faculty 190

Amount of Fees and Date of Payment £8. 8. — [illegible] 18. VI. 05

Part Two: Isaac Rosenberg in Heaven

A sentence from the great work of Jewish mysticism, the Zohar, stands out in the Joseph Hertz anthology, *A Book of Jewish Thoughts*, which Jennie Salaman Cohen sent Rosenberg at the front in the summer of1917: "There are halls in the heavens above that open but to the voice of song". Perhaps Isaac read those words, perhaps he didn't. Either way, he became his own words and went directly to that particular heaven where, we may suppose, poets discuss, with or without anxiety, those they have influenced and those who have influenced them. This is their chance to speak freely. Having crossed the bar, they can talk even to Shakespeare, face to face. Location, wrote Eudora Welty, is the crossroads of circumstance. So is time. Location and occasion, time and space, converge in heaven.

The Poets' Paradise this is
To which but few can come;
The Muses' only bower of bliss
Their dear Elysium.

– Michael Drayton (quoted by Harold Bloom)

SCENE ONE FROM NOBODY'S ROMEO

(Literary Exchanges in Heaven)

John Keats:

Good morning, Isaac. It's been a long time since we had a chat. I've been looking at your poems again. Don't think I didn't notice your allusion to my 'Belle Dame Sans Merci' in 'From France': "And some birds sing". A beautiful poem.

Isaac Rosenberg:

Thank you, John. Yes, the echo was intentional. On the other hand, the larks in my 'Returning, We Hear the Larks' do not consciously allude to your own lark in 'Fancy'. I'm glad you like 'From France': it is not often mentioned in the literature on me, which I note is exponentially burgeoning.

John Keats:

Ah yes, your hidden rhyme: "lurks" and "larks". I salute you, brother. The pun is as good as Shakespeare's "torture" and "torch", which occur together in a single line in *Antony and Cleopatra.* As for exponentially burgeoning, isn't burgeoning always exponential? Isaac, my dear, that was a tautology.

Isaac Rosenberg:

Point taken! The literature on you burgeoned exponentially in 2019, the bicentenary of your greatest poems. I wonder if there were any celebrations in 1919. I was already dead. Tell me, John, did you write 'Ode to a Nightingale' at the Spaniards Inn or Wentworth Place? The critics disagree.

John Keats:

I don't know about celebrations but, no question, I wrote it at

Wentworth Place in 1819 or, proleptically speaking, in the house on Keats Grove, as it was renamed on January 1, 1910. A couple of years later you were living at 32 Carlingford Road, ten minutes away.

Isaac Rosenberg:

"Thou was not born for death, immortal bird"…. Birds and English poetry. Everywhere. Crows and ravens, owls and hawks, nightingales and (sky) larks.

Keats and Rosenberg in unison:

"It was the nightingale and not the lark".

John Keats:

Great minds speak alike. I saw John Clare the other day, which sadly for both of us never happened when we were alive. He speaks frankly. He says that I am a city boy, that my descriptions of nature derive from my fancy, and that my nightingale is in a long tradition of poetic nightingales, whereas his 'Nightingale's Nest' is grounded in natural history. My problem with him is, appropriately enough, the opposite: sometimes description prevails over sentiment. He wrote to our shared publisher that he would heed my critique. By the way, his doctors, like mine, thought that poetry was bad for him. Indeed, he told Taylor, the publisher, that my symptoms were alarming. John Clare remembers one occasion, in Taylor's office, scribbling down revisions of a poem on the back of one of my letters. I told him it was sweet of him to write the memorial sonnet, but that it was not one of his best poems. He agrees and says simply that he could not find words to meet the occasion. We are planning to go for a long walk – like Charles Lamb and other friends of Coleridge in 'This Lime Tree Bower, our Prison' while the man himself, who had hurt his foot, stayed at home and wrote the poem. And what a poem.

Isaac Rosenberg:

Yes, friendship with other men is so important. But what about women? John, you were Fanny Braun's Romeo. I was nobody's Romeo. What other birds are there in Shakespeare? Magpie, starling, dove, wren, chough, Does Phoenix count? The rook, the lark, the eagle and others in *Cymbeline*.

Shelley:

I couldn't help overhearing this conversation. You listened well to the music in my ode. There's an allusion to my lark in Hart Crane's amazing 'Bridge', but there is certainly no allusion to John's lark in your poem, Isaac.

Isaac Rosenberg:

Quite right, Shelley. Ah, you were a year older than me when you died, but you, John, you were younger, although older than Keith Douglas, who addresses me directly in a poem. There's an honoured member of our club.

Keith Douglas:

Bonjour my brothers. "The spirit drank the café lights", as Isaac writes in 'From France'.

Isaac Rosenberg:

Keith, my friend, thank you. Of course, you too have included a bird, a hawk, in the poem where you kindly apostrophise me.

Keith Douglas:

Yes indeed. You know Ted Hughes's crows of course. He edited a selection of my work just before starting to write those amazing poems. Ted's hawk came earlier but it has nothing to do with mine. While we're on the subject of birds, remember Bede's sparrow?

Isaac Rosenberg:

Of course I do. A bird it never was. Then there's Edward Thomas's 'Unknown Bird' and the famous blackbird in Adlestrop. Edward died a year before me, almost to the day, not five miles from where I fell. I bet he's somewhere around, chewing the cud with his friend Robert Frost.

Keith Douglas:

Look, there's Jon Silkin talking to Sidney Keyes, who seems to be trying to get away. Probably has a date with the other poets who died in the war, Alun Lewis, John Jarmain and Timothy Corsellis. By the way, Silkin has a Hebrew-speaking bird in his poem 'Two Freedoms'.

Isaac Rosenberg:

Enough about war and enough about birds. Jon Silkin wrote a lot about me, he even called me a "lion-tongued enabling angel"! People say I influenced his diction.

Keith Douglas:

Jon! Come here! Have you met John Keats, Percy Shelley, Isaac Rosenberg? Tell us about Isaac's diction.

Jon Silkin:

Respectful salutations to you all. Isaac, we meet at last. I have some questions for you, and answers, but we have plenty of time in the world, here and now, *af yener velt*, as living Jews used to say.

Isaac Rosenberg:

The next world…. Jon, fire away, to coin a phrase. I see you speak Yiddish.

Jon Silkin

A bisl. It was not the language of my childhood, unlike yours. If I'd been in the war, I'd have been one of the Bantams. One of the questions I have always wanted to ask you, Isaac, is about your languages. I know you speak fluent Yiddish, but how good is your Hebrew?

Isaac Rosenberg:

Well, I spoke Yiddish all the time as a child but my Hebrew is almost non-existent. I know some of the prayers and the bible portion I read at my barmitzvah and a few phrases, but that's all. Why?

Jon Silkin:

I was talking to Avigdor Hameiri and Uri Zvi Greenberg, two Hebrew poets fighting on the other side, who started out as Yiddish poets. They don't speak English so Yehuda Amichai served as interpreter. You could have done it if you'd been there. Yehuda had to work hard to calm them down when they got into a row about the history of Jewish settlement in the Yishuv. But they were friends in real life, despite major political disagreements. I overheard Avigdor and Uri Zvi talking to the Angel of Death and the Angel of Lost Causes. Hebrew is the language spoken by the angels, so we'd better start taking lessons from Avigdor and Uri Zvi if we want to communicate with these messengers.

John Keats:

I'm more interested in Hampstead than in angels, although I once visited the Angel Islington and my brother Tom is buried in Bunhill Fields, near William Blake, who consorted with angels. Let's imagine for a moment we're in Hampstead, Isaac. I mentioned Wentworth Place before and your own address, Carlingford Road.

Isaac Rosenberg

You take me back.

John Keats

They're both close to my first place in Well Walk, next door the pub, a few doors down from Constable's own house, although we never lived in the street at the same time. But the house I lived in has been demolished. A local estate agent persists in saying that I lived in the house presently numbered 46, to the annoyance of the curators at Wentworth Place. At that end of Well Walk, there are two now large block of flats on the edge of the Heath, built long after I died. They're close to where I saw Constable walking home from a work session – but I didn't speak to him. Jon, your mate Ken Smith – a fine poet – told me you sold copies of *Stand* in the William pub on Hampstead High Street and the Everyman cinema queue. I heard that you also sold copies to students on Kings Parade in Cambridge and to a young poet, one Lucas, on Cork Street in London.

Jon Silkin

That's right. We were hands on. It's all very well enjoying the editorial side, but what's the point if no copies are sold?

John Keats

But Keith, you never lived in London.

Keith Douglas:

Quite right. I'd have visited your house later on, when it was opened to the public.

Shelley:

Coleridge met Constable once, but in the Lake District not in Hampstead.

Keith Douglas:

I'd love to have been a fly on the wall when that conversation took place.

Jon Silkin:

If it was a conversation! I wonder if Coleridge has changed since he arrived here. Perhaps he has recovered the brilliance of his prime. Ah, a mind as regal as that of Coleridge overthrown by the treachery of his own will and by the conspiracy of himself against himself: I quote De Quincey from memory. Hey, there's Edward Thomas. Robert Frost has just left him. Probably heading for Walt Whitman.

Edward Thomas:

Greetings. Coleridge was holding forth just now. I tried to ask him about the ancient mariner but he insisted on talking about Wordsworth and the poets' daughters, Dora and Sara, who were friends. The Coleridge girl later lived at 27 Downshire Hill, very close to your second place in Hampstead, John, and not so far from your first. Those girls: one with a father who was never there, the other with a father who was always there. Fathers and daughters, that's a subject for poetry. And what about *Fathers and Sons*? I read somewhere that Turgenev got the idea for his great novel while on holiday in Ventnor. Also that he met Tennyson, but not in Ventnor. And look, here's Wilfred Owen.

Isaac Rosenberg

Talk of the devil, or rather God: I'm referring to Wilfred's 'Parable of the Old Man and the Young', Abraham and Isaac, the binding of Isaac, the *Akeda*. Wilfred, I have a bone to pick with you. "The poetry is in the pity", you wrote in your preface. I agree with Geoffrey Hill, in his Oxford lecture, that the poetry is not in the pity, rather that the pity is registered in the poetry, but he over-states the case against you and I regret it, even though he goes on to make a case for me, I can't deny it.

Wilfred Owen

To say Hill over-states is an understatement concerning his gloss on 'Anthem for Doomed Youth' and the parable you refer to. He says my preface is simple-minded, and that it is an intellectual and emotional self-betrayal, and that it undermines my poetry. That is strong language. For a start, he could have made allowances for the circumstances. He went over the top, to use a phrase that started life in our war. Going over the top carries risks. I should have a chat with him, but he's been busy talking to Eliot and Gurney, so it would be a kindness, albeit undeserved, to give him a break. A line from my late poem 'The Roads Also' – "And the dead scribble on walls" – reminds him of Keith Douglas, who apostrophised you, not me. Yeats too is on my list of poets to argue with, if I can tear him away from the Tarot pack and the Ouija board. Whether or not he really believed that stuff, he was sillier than us, if I may amend Auden's phrase in the elegy. I like Yeats's poems much more than he likes mine. But his argument in the preface to the Oxford anthology makes no sense. He goes on to describe me in a letter as 'all blood, dirt and sucked sugar stick'......and, don't forget, he described you as being "all windy rhetoric". He was a great poet but he had no gift to set a poet right. Ho hum, I'd rather talk about cricket. Remember Jessie Pope: "They'll take the Kaiser's middle wicket / And smash it by clean British Cricket". I was browsing in Wisden before going to France: In 1899, A.E.J Collins of Clifton College made 628 runs, the highest recorded score in cricket until an Indian lad surpassed it in 2016. Mind you, it was not a first class game, but even so. Did you know that Douglas Haig and Henry Newbolt were at Clifton together? Henry's war poem, 'Vitaï Lampada', is at the same time a cricket poem and an Empire poem. It was published in 1892. I wonder if young Collins read it. Poor boy, he died very early in the war, November 1914.

All together

There's a breathless hush in the close tonight
Ten to make and the last man in…

Henry Newbolt

Thank you. The close is Clifton College Close, where we played cricket and Collins scored his runs. Yes, I knew Douglas Haig at school. He probably appreciated Jessie's doggerel. I'm touched that you fellows recited my poem. I have written other poems, you know. 'Drake's Drum', for example, and 'The Fighting Temeraire'. But the one everyone remembers is 'Vitaï Lampada'. It's quoted on a relief carving at Lords in Wellington Road, which you can see from the bus.

All together

But the voice of a schoolboy rallies the ranks:
'Play up! play up! and play the game!'

Isaac Rosenberg

Just occurred to me: my old Hebrew teacher, Joseph Polack, might have been watching while Collins scored all those runs. Polack taught at Clifton.

Henry Newbolt

Did you know my great grandfather was Samuel Solomon, the quack doctor who patented a famous quack remedy, the so-called 'Balm of Gilead'?

Isaac Rosenberg

I wonder if he was an ancestor of Solomon Joseph Solomon, your exact contemporary?

Jon Silkin

Marianne Moore! Elizabeth Bishop! An honour to meet you. We met in another place, if I'm not mistaken. It's about time some women came on board in this celestial ship of fools. Let's stop our male grandstanding.

John Keats

Speak for yourself, Jon. Introduce me to Miss Bishop. She and I shall discuss moths and mournful psyches.

APPENDIX 1

After completing this essay, I discovered a truly remarkable book of poems, *Salient*, by Elizabeth T. Gray, with an afterword by Nathaniel Tarn. A long poem that works by fragment and collage, *Salient* is a visionary, lyrical and sometimes mystical exploration of the Third Battle of Ypres, better known as Passchendaele. The poem is one of the very rare literary works by a non-combatant in, on and about the material and psychic territory of World War One (as is, in the context of World War Two, and specifically the Battle of Britain, Nathaniel Tarn's own equally impressive and powerful *Avia*). Extrospective and objective/objectivist, *Salient* contains high emotion through technique and vision – essential components of morality, including protection against frisson – and recovers the landscape as [back] story, as well as the technologies of war (including camouflage) and the passages of death. *Salient* moves us to reflection on the deeds and works of men. Poetry by non-combatants about war (or about the camps by those who were not in one) demands the highest standards of care and respect. I believe that Isaac Rosenberg would have saluted these works as a precious contribution to the poetry of war. I hope to write about Gray and Tarn on a later occasion.

PS Harold Bloom, in his valedictory book, *Take Arms against a Sea of Troubles*, sends us back to the powerful, austere and moving poem 'Death of a Soldier' by Wallace Stevens, published in *Harmonium* in 1923.

APPENDIX 2

I went to the Special Collections in University College London to look at Rosenberg's entry [see illlustrations] in the Roll of Honour of UCL members, which of course includes students from the Slade School of Fine Art. While there I looked at the mainly unpublished manuscript diaries of the painter Willie Townsend, a much loved and greatly respected teacher at the school, who had been the tutor of Paula Rego and many of her friends and colleagues. Thanks to the workings of serendipity, I was pleased to find the following entry on March 11, 1960, which refers to an exhibition that came on to UCL from Leeds University, curated by Jon Silkin and Maurice de Sausmarez.

We have an exhibition of paintings and drawings by Isaac Rosenberg, the poet, who was a Slade student from 1911 to 1913, hanging in the Reading Room. There are three self-portraits which are well constructed and firmly painted and perceptive and thoroughly good by any standards of English portraiture of the period. These are by far the best things; his few composition drawings are period pieces. Andrew Forge laid on a small reception for people to to meet his [Rosenberg's] sister, Mrs Wynik, who spends her life doing what she can for his work and reputation. Some of the staff, others from the college, J. Isaacs and a few others stayed on to meet them to Victoria and home.

In the Slade records of Isaac Rosenberg, I think that under "C" (ladies), one can see Carrington (Dora) and Brett (Dorothy). Rosenberg was registered for Life Drawing Full Time.

APPENDIX 3

21 April 2021: on my first outing since lockdown restrictions have been relaxed, I went to the British Library to check out a book by Benvenuta Solomon (see bibliography) which I learned about in a Blackwells rare books catalogue. The catalogue alerts one to a couple of "powerful" war poems, 'Searchlights (January 1915)' and 'New Year, 1918'. Intrigued by her surname (was she a member of the family?) as well by as the subject matter, I ended up disappointed. Like those of Jennie Salaman Cohen, the poems are conventional and patriotic, "flag-days", as Rosenberg said sharply of Brooke's work. From 'Searchlights': "Life is the least thing man must sacrifice /Ere peace shall come again" and from 'New Year, 1918': "Now let our hearts be lifted to the height / Of those who died for England". The *Jewish Chronicle* archives reveal mention of two women named Benvenuta Solomon, but no hint of other members of her family, so connection is impossible to establish.

Another Solomon, Gilbert Solomon, who was at the Slade with Isaac Rosenberg and then served in the RAF in World War One – becoming a second lieutenant in the Royal Flying Corps and a Captain in the RAF – was a cousin of Ruth Löwy and a nephew of Solomon J. Solomon. It is pleasing that he followed his uncle into camouflage, becoming art director of the Design Section of Civilian Camouflage at Leamington during World War Two. His uncle's techniques were still being deployed. We learn from Gilbert's Slade record that he was living in the family home in West Hampstead when he was a student. Unlike Rosenberg, he was not poor.

ACKNOWLEDGMENTS AND THANKS

To Elizabeth Cook for her valuable comments by phone and email after we exchanged early draft essays on Rosenberg. And for her equally valuable later comments on the penultimate draft, including drawing my attention to Geoffrey Hill's Oxford Lectures as Professor of Poetry. She knows when to be tactful and when to be forthright.

To Jean Liddiard, sounding-board incarnate, for various discussions and encouragement.

To Rachel Dickson and Sarah MacDougall of the Ben-Uri Gallery for digging out their article on Isaac Rosenberg and to Sarah MacDougall for supplying a PDF of a catalogue I had mislaid. To Sarah MacDougall, again, for discussion of *Self-Portrait with a Steel Helmet* and links to articles about the Solomon family; also, for help in accessing the 1920 Yiddish magazine *Renesans*, as suggested by David Mazower. To Julia Weiner – long associated with Ben-Uri – who helped me with archive material.

To Miriam Neiger-Fleischmann for discussing her thesis on Avigdor Hameiri and her unpublished paper on the meeting between Hameiri and Sutzkever, and for co-translating Hameiri's poems (and Sutzkever's) and, especially, for researching – by design and also by accident – the 'wood-lark'.

To Jim McCue for help with the full quote about Rosenberg from Eliot's article in *The Criterion.* To Bernard Wynick and Shelley Swade of Rosenberg's family for reminiscences.

To Nathaniel Tarn for putting me in touch with Elizabeth Gray and to her for putting me in touch with Paul Reed, and to Paul Reed for comments on Solomon J. Solomon and for finding his index card. To John Lucas for his comments on two drafts and in particular for a discussion about Ivor Gurney.

To Tony Flynn for germane comments, including a suggestive comparison with Simone Weil in relation to my epigraph from Rosenberg.

To Peter Redman for encouraging focused attention on certain details of World War One and, in particular, a discussion about *Gas*, Gyula Zilzer's folio of lithographs about gas warfare, now in his possession.

To John Matthias for allowing me to read in advance of publication his book *Some Words on those Wars*, which touches on my own preoccupations.

To Susan Saffer, for kindness and for discussions about footnoting and other details. To Colin Shindler for his patience concerning archive access.

To Una Summerson for photographing the John Parr pavement and to Fred Beake for photocopying the article by Charles Hobday.

To Andy Stahl at the Slade, and Daniel Mitchell and Robert Winckworth at UCL Libraries Record Office/Special Collections for help with the records of Isaac Rosenberg and Gilbert Solomon, in the public domain and private. For William Townsend's manuscript diaries: copyright UCL Special Collections, with thanks for permission to publish an extract from the restricted access work; also thanks to the William Townsend estate in the person of his daughter Charlotte Townsend-Gault, for permission to publish.

To Dr C.S.Knighton of Clifton College archives and the staff in the National Gallery library. To Stephanie Lafferty for "devilling" in the *ODNB*. To the Tower Hamlets local history library in Bancroft Road.

To John Taylor, the late Elaine Feinstein, Jon Glover, Jean Moorcroft Wilson, Geoffrey Alderman, Glenda Abramson, Deborah Maccoby, Michael Schmidt and W.D. Jackson for discussions on specific points.

To Olwen Stocker and the estate of Peter Paul Piech for his two prints of Isaac Rosenberg.

To Paula Rego, for encouragement and enthusiasm.

To Christopher Ricks, for paying me the compliment of hoping that my book will persuade him to change his mind about Rosenberg.

To Frank Auerbach for his letter dated 14 September, 2021.

To Nathanael and Rachael Ravenlock (Shoestring's typesetters and designers), and not for the first time.

If any copyright permission has not been obtained, my apologies. This will be rectified in future editions.

BOOKS, ARTICLES AND WEBSITES CONSULTED OR REFERRED TO

Abramson, Glenda, *Hebrew Writing of the First World War*, 2008, Vallentine Mitchell

Akers, Geoff, *Beating for Light: The Story of Isaac Rosenberg*, 2006, Juniper Books

Bate, Jonathan, *Bright Star, Green Light: The Beautiful Works and Damned Lives of John Keats and F. Scott Fitzgerald*, 2021, William Collins

Bate, Jonathan, *John Clare*, 2004, Picador

Bloom, Harold, *Take Arms against a Sea of Troubles: The Power of the Reader's Mind over a Universe of Death*, 2020, Yale University Press

Carr, J. L., *A Month in the Country*, 2000, Penguin Classics

Cohen, Joseph, *Journey to the Trenches: The Life of Isaac Rosenberg* 1890–2018, 1975, Robson Books

Cook, Elizabeth, 'Isaac Rosenberg: A Poet to Paint a Poet', 2018–2021, unpublished essay, forthcoming in *Stand*

Cook, Elizabeth, 'From Pandemonium' (review of Noakes, 2004, see Noakes below), 2005, *London Review of Books*, 27/17, September

Cook, Elizabeth (ed), *John Keats: The Major Works*, 2008, Oxford World Classics

Dickson, Rachel and MacDougall, Sarah, 'Isaac Rosenberg and the Whitehall Madonna', 2008, *Jewish Quarterly*, number 55:1, pp 61–3

Dickson, Rachel and MacDougall, Sarah, *Whitechapel at War: Isaac Rosenberg and his Circle*, 2008, Lund Humphries

Dobson, Barrie, *The Jews of Medieval York and the Massacre of March 1190*, 1974, Borthwick Papers, York

Eliot, T.S., *The Poems* (two volumes), edited by Christopher Ricks and Jim McCue, 2015, Faber and Faber

Glover, Jon and Silkin, Jon, *The Penguin Book of First World War Prose*, 1989, Viking

Gray, Elizabeth T., *Salient* (with an Afterword by Nathaniel Tarn), 2020, New Directions

Gray, Elizabeth T., 'Coming in on a Wing and a Lyre: Nathaniel Tarn's *Avid*', February 2019, issue of *Dispatches from the Poetry Wars*
Gurney, Ivor, *Collected Poems* (edited by P.J. Kavanagh), 1982, Oxford University Press
Hameiri, Avigdor (trs. Jacob Freedman), *The Great Madness*, 1951, Vantage Press
Hameiri, Avigdor (trs Peter Appelbaum, with introduction by Avner Holtzman), *Hell on Earth*, 2017, Wayne State University Press
Hertz, J. H. (ed), *A Book of Jewish Thoughts*, 1920, Oxford University Press
Hill, Geoffrey, *Collected Critical Writings*, 2009, Oxford University Press
Hill, Geoffrey, *Oxford Lectures on Poetry*, 2010–2015 (available online). [The one relevant to my text is dated December 2, 2014–15]
Hobday, Charles, 'Isaac Rosenberg, Revolutionary Poet', 2000, *London Magazine*, 40 (3/4)
Hobday, Charles, *Edgell Rickword, A Poet at War*, 1989, Carcanet Press
Jacobs, A.C., *Nameless Country: Selected Poems*, 2018, Northern House/Carcanet
Jones, David, *In Parenthesis*, 1937, Faber and Faber
Jones, David, *Wedding Poems*, 2002 Enitharmon
Keery, James, *Apocalypse: An Anthology*, 2021, Carcanet
Kulka, Otto Dov, *Landscapes of the Metropolis of Death*, 2014, Penguin
Lawson, Peter, *Anglo-Jewish Poetry from Isaac Rosenberg to Elaine Feinstein*, 2006, Vallentine Mitchell
Leftwich, Joseph, *Diary 1911/1912* (unpublished), copy in Tower Hamlets Local History Library
Leftwich, Joseph, *Israel Zangwill and Isaac Rosenberg*, annual lecture at Writers from the East End conference, probably 1976
[Joseph Leftwich], *Joseph Leftwich at Eighty Five*, (ed., S.J. Goldsmith), 1978, Federation of Jewish Relief Organisations
Liddiard, Jean, *Isaac Rosenberg: The Half Used Life*, 1975, Victor Gollancz

Liddiard, Jean, *Isaac Rosenberg: Selected Poems and Letters*, 2003, Enitharmon Press

Liddiard, Jean, *Poetry out of my Head and Heart: Selected Letters of Isaac Rosenberg*, 2007, Enitharmon Press. (This book includes Annie Wynick's memoir of her brother).

Liddiard, Jean, 'Isaac Rosenberg: A Personal View of his Reputation since 1918, with an Unpublished Letter to Paul Nash', 2010, *The War Poetry Review* (Journal of the War Poets Association), Volume 1 Number 2

Lipke, William, *David Bomberg: A Critical Study of his Life and Work*, 1968, Adams & Dart

Lowery, Owen, *A Critical and Creative Examination of the 'Extrospective' Poetry of Keith Douglas,* 2016, University of Bolton

Lowery, Owen, *The Crash Wake Poems*, 2021, Carcanet Press (and other books)

Lucas, John, 'The Commonwealth of Toil' (on the sanity of Ivor Gurney), 2020, *Raceme* 9 (June/July)

Maccoby, Deborah, *God Made Blind: Isaac Rosenberg: His Life and Poetry*, 1999, Symposium Press

Malraux, André, *Les Noyers de l'Altenburg*, 1948, Gallimard

Malraux, André, *Lazare*, 1974, Gallimard

Manne, Robert, 2021, *Jewish Quarterly*, number 244, page 126

Matthias, John, *Some Words on those Wars*, 2021, Dos Madres Press

Milosz, Czeslaw, *The Witness of Poetry*, 1983, Harvard University Press

Neiger-Fleischmann, Miriam, *From the Abyss of Limbo: The Poetry of Avigdor Hameiri, from its Beginnings to the Publication of Sefer Hashirim in 1933*, PhD, 2015, Hebrew University of Jerusalem.

Noakes, Vivien, *Isaac Rosenberg*, 2008, Oxford University Press (21st Century Oxford Authors)

Noakes, Vivien, *The Poems and Plays of Isaac Rosenberg*, 2004, Oxford University Press

Parsons, Ian, *The Collected Works of Isaac Rosenberg*, 1984, Chatto and Windus

Pound, Ezra, *ABC of Reading*, 1951, Faber and Faber

Rakosi, Carl, 'Message to the Symposiasts', 1981/2, issue of *Stand* 23.1

Rankin, Nicholas, *Churchill's Wizards: The British Genius for Deception*, 2009, Faber & Faber

Remarque, Erich Maria, *All Quiet on the Western Front*, 1929 (1996, Vintage)

Reznikoff, Charles, *The Lionhearted* (a Story About the Jews of Medieval England), 1944, The Jewish Publication Society of America

Rickword, Edgell, *Behind the Eyes* (Collected Poems and Translations), 1976, Carcanet Press

Roe, Nicholas, *John Keats*, 2012, Yale University Press

Rudolf, Anthony and Schwartz, Howard (eds), *Voices Within the Ark: the Modern Jewish Poets*, 1980, Avon Books

Rudolf, Anthony, *At an Uncertain Hour: Primo Levi's War against Oblivion*, 1990, Menard Press. [Note: In this book I referenced Richard Rubenstein's *The Cunning of History*, 1978, Harper Perennial, and Arthur Cohen's *The Tremendum: A Theological Interpretation of the Holocaust*, 1981, Continuum. Cohen's book contains a valuable neologism: "sub-scend". He writes: "If there is no transcendence beyond the abyss [of the death camps], the abyss must be inspected further.... The abyss must be *sub-scended*, penetrated to its perceivable depths", and he proceeds to a discussion of the atomic bomb. Meanwhile, I await the completion of Mark Levene's work-in-progress, *Essays for End Time.* Also, I would like to mention my edition of Piotr Rawicz's *Blood from the Sky*, 2004, Elliott and Thompson, and my article 'Ka-Tzetnik 135633,' in Sorrel Kerbel, Muriel Emanuel and Laura Phillips (eds.), *Jewish Writers of the Twentieth Century*, 2003, Routledge]

Rudolf, Anthony, 'F.T. Prince Supplement', 2002, special issue of *Poetry Nation Review*, no. 147

Rudolf, Anthony, 'Paths Of Peace: A Personal Trajectory', 2007 (in *A Time to Speak Out: Independent Jewish Voices*, edited by Anne Karpf, Brian Klug, Jacqueline Rose and Barbara Rosenbaum), *Verso*

Rudolf, Anthony, *Zigzag*, 2010, Carcanet Press

Rudolf. Anthony, 'Rescue Work: Memory and Text', 2004, *Stand* volume 5 (3) and its sequel, 'Obstinate Hope', 2021, *Paideuma* (special issue on literature and war)

Schmidt, Michael, *Lives of the Poets*, 1998, Weidenfeld and Nicholson

Searle, Chris, *Isaac and I: A life in Poetry*, 2017, Five Leaves

Searle, Chris, *Whitechapel Boys: A Reading of the Poetry of Isaac Rosenberg*, 2018, Communimedia

Silkin, Jon, *Out of Battle: Poetry of the Great War*, 1972, Oxford University Press

Silkin, Jon, *Collected Poems*, 2015, Northern House/Carcanet

Simpson, Matt, 'Only a living thing – some notes towards a reading of Isaac Rosenberg's 'Break of Day in the Trenches', in *Critical Survey: Writing and the First World War*, (Volume 2, number 2, edited by Bryan Loughrey)

Sinclair, Iain and Lichtenstein, Rachel, *Rodinsky's Room* (paperback edition containing post-script), 2000, Granta

Solomon, Benvenuta, *The Tower Unbuilded*, 1922, Blackwells

Tarn, Nathaniel, *Avia*, 2008, Shearsman

Tomlinson, Charles, *Isaac Rosenberg of Bristol*, 1982, The Historical Association, Bristol

Tomlinson, Charles, 'Fate and the Image of Music: an Examination of Rosenberg's Plays', 1974, *Poetry Nation* 3

Townsend, William, *Townsend Journals: An Artist's Record of His Times, 1928–51* (edited by Andrew Forge), 1976, Tate Gallery

Vansittart, Peter, *Voices from the Great War*, 1981, Jonathan Cape

Welty, Eudora, *One Writer's Beginnings*, 1984, Harvard University Press

Willing, Victoria, *Spring Offensive*, 2017, Clapham Omnibus

Wilson, Jean Moorcroft, *Isaac Rosenberg: Poet and Painter*, 1975, Cecil Woolf

Wilson, Jean Moorcroft, *Isaac Rosenberg: The Making of a Great War Poet*, 2007, Weidenfeld and Nicholson

Winterbottom, Derek, *Dynasty: The Polack Family and the Jewish House at Clifton*, 2008, Polack's House Educational Trust

Zilzer, Gyula, *Gas* (twenty four lithographs), with a foreword by Romain Rolland, 1932, Editions du Phare, Paris

ONLINE

Still, Colin, "Letters from the Trenches", 2021, www.opticnerve.co.uk

https://www.birds.org.il/he/species-page/366/species-description

Solomon, Solomon J., *Wikipedia* entry. [The Solomon family tree on the genealogy website *Geni* makes an egregious error about the death date of Henrietta Löwy]

HM Government, *Global Britain in a Competitive Age* (Integrated Review of Security, Defence, Development and Foreign Policy), 2021

[Today, once again, we are entering perilous times in the territory of nuclear risk and moving further along the pathway that began in World War One. Little by little the concept of nuclear war that can be fought in a limited way is gaining ground.

The UK is lowering the threshold in terms of deterrence. The recent government review talks of circumstances in which the response to an "emerging technology" deployed by a non-nuclear country would be nuclear weapons. The number of warheads for Trident is to be increased, and no explanation given. This is unilateralism, unilateral nuclear rearmament, a reckless regression, even for a Tory government.

In general, the lengthy official document is mind-blowingly grandiose in its ambition and self-deception. We are gearing ourselves up to take on the Russians. Rosenberg would have laughed his head off, and then, like the angels in *Measure for Measure*, wept. It is to be hoped that President Biden will find it in his mind and heart to undemonise Russia and engage in genuine diplomacy to reduce the real risk of nuclear war, perhaps by misadventure.

The Doomsday Clock of the Bulletin of Atomic Scientists at the University of Chicago stands at 100 seconds to midnight. And what am I/are we doing about it? In its response to the review, the Labour Party, spooked by charges of so-called unilateral disarmament, avoided the real issues. When the crisis comes, they will be judged complicit, and it will be too late. "Ye ken the noo".]

25 February, 1916

The war is indeed becoming violent. Perhaps, who knows, these are its death throes.

26 August, 1916

I fear it will go on for another three years. Very, very distressing.

Guillaume Apollinaire

Lettres à Madeleine: Tendre comme le souvenir, ed. Lawrence Campa, 2005, Gallimard

(*Letters to Madeleine* translated by Donald Nicholson-Smith, 2018, Seagull Books)